GOOGLE CALENDAR

FOR BEGINNERS

The Comprehensive Guide To Bettering Your Time-Management And Scheduling, Organizing Your Schedule And Coordinating Events To Improve Your Productivity

GOOGLE CALENDAR FOR BEGINNERS

The Comprehensive Guide To Bettering Your Time-Management And Scheduling, Organizing Your Schedule And Coordinating Events To Improve Your Productivity

GOOGLE CALENDAR FOR BEGINNERS: THE COMPREHENSIVE GUIDE TO BETTERING YOUR TIME-MANAGEMENT AND SCGEDULING, ORGANIZING YOUR SCHEDULE AND COORDINATING EVENTS TO IMPROVE YOUR PRODUCTIVITY

First edition. November 27, 2023.

Written by Voltaire Lumiere.

TABLE OF CONTENTS

CHAPTER 1
INTRODUCTION TO GOOGLE CALENDAR

- **Why Use Google Calendar?**

Google Calendar is a dynamic digital scheduling tool designed to revolutionize the way individuals manage their time and organize their commitments. This cloud-based service, seamlessly integrated into the Google ecosystem, offers a host of features that cater to diverse user needs.

At its core, Google Calendar serves as a centralized hub for scheduling and organizing events, appointments, and tasks. Its user-friendly interface and intuitive design make navigation effortless, ensuring accessibility for users of all technological proficiencies.

Why Use Google Calendar?

1. **Effortless Integration:** Google Calendar seamlessly integrates with other Google services, such as Gmail, Google Meet, and Google Drive. This interconnected ecosystem fosters a unified digital workspace, enhancing overall productivity.

2. **Dynamic and Real-Time Updates:** The platform goes beyond traditional calendars by providing dynamic features. Real-

time updates, automated reminders, and the ability to set recurring events ensure that users stay ahead of their commitments without the risk of oversights.

3. **Collaborative Efficiency:** Google Calendar promotes collaboration by allowing users to share calendars with colleagues, friends, or family. Features like event invitations and integrated video conferencing through Google Meet facilitate efficient coordination and communal organization.

4. **Accessibility Anytime, Anywhere:** Being a cloud-based service, Google Calendar ensures accessibility from any device with internet connectivity. Whether at the desk, commuting, or away from the office, users can manage their schedules seamlessly.

5. **Flexibility and Adaptability:** The platform adapts to the fast-paced nature of modern life, offering features that transcend the limitations of traditional paper calendars. Users can efficiently manage their time, adapt to changing schedules, and optimize productivity.

In conclusion, Google Calendar is not just a scheduling tool; it is a strategic decision to embrace efficiency, organization, and collaboration in the digital age. Its integration, dynamic features, collaborative capabilities, accessibility, and adaptability make it an indispensable resource for individuals and professionals seeking to optimize their time-management practices and enhance overall productivity.

- **Overview of Key Features**

Google Calendar boasts a robust array of features designed to elevate your scheduling and organizational experience. These functionalities go beyond mere date-tracking, providing users with a versatile toolkit to streamline their daily lives.

1. **Event Customization:** Tailor your events with precision. Google Calendar allows you to add detailed information, including event titles, locations, descriptions, and customizable reminders. This ensures that each entry is rich with context and tailored to your unique needs.

2. **Intuitive Interface:** Navigating through your calendar is a seamless experience. The intuitive design allows for effortless exploration, event creation, and adjustment of settings. The platform's user-friendly layout ensures a smooth interaction for users at any level of technological familiarity.

3. **Color-Coding for Organization:** Visual clarity is paramount. Google Calendar enables users to color-code events, providing a quick and effective way to categorize and distinguish between different types of commitments. This visual organization enhances at-a-glance understanding.

4. **Recurring Events and Reminders:** Efficiency meets flexibility. Whether it's a weekly meeting or a monthly reminder, Google Calendar empowers users to set up recurring events with ease. Customizable reminders ensure that crucial tasks and appointments are never overlooked.

5. **Seamless Integration with Google Services:** Benefit from a seamlessly interconnected digital experience. Google Calendar integrates effortlessly with other Google services such as Gmail, Google Meet, and Google Drive. This integration enhances overall productivity by consolidating your digital workspace.

6. **Multi-View Options:** Tailor your perspective. Google Calendar offers daily, weekly, and monthly views, allowing users to choose the timeframe that best suits their planning needs. Custom views and filters further enhance the adaptability of the platform.

7. **Collaborative Features:** Foster teamwork and coordination. Users can easily share entire calendars, invite others to events, and manage permissions collaboratively. The inclusion of collaborative scheduling tools and integration with Google Meet facilitates efficient group organization.

8. **Task Integration:** Seamlessly blend your to-dos with your schedule. Google Calendar integrates tasks and to-do lists, allowing users to create, organize, and prioritize tasks within the same

platform. This integration promotes a holistic approach to time management.

In essence, the key features of Google Calendar are meticulously crafted to provide users with a versatile and intuitive scheduling experience, fostering efficiency, organization, and adaptability in the digital realm.

- **Setting Up Your Google Calendar Account**

Embarking on the journey of efficient time management starts with the establishment of your Google Calendar account. This process is straightforward, ensuring that you can swiftly transition into the realm of organized scheduling. Here's a concise guide to setting up your Google Calendar account:

1. **Google Account Creation:** If you don't have a Google Account, the first step is to create one. Navigate to the Google Account creation page, provide the required information, and follow the prompts to set up your account. If you already have a Google Account, proceed to the next step.

2. **Accessing Google Calendar:** Once your Google Account is active, access Google Calendar by visiting the dedicated webpage or through the Google Apps menu (represented by a grid of dots) on the top-right corner of most Google services.

3. **Initial Calendar Configuration:** Upon entering Google Calendar, you may be prompted to configure some initial settings.

This includes selecting your time zone, preferred date and time formats, and other basic preferences. Ensure these settings align with your personal preferences for a tailored experience.

4. **Customizing Calendar Appearance:** Make your calendar visually appealing and easy to navigate. Customize the color scheme and choose between different calendar views (day, week, month) based on your preferred visual organization style.

5. **Adding Additional Calendars (Optional):** Google Calendar allows users to create multiple calendars for different purposes. This is particularly useful for segregating personal and professional commitments. You can add additional calendars based on your needs, such as a work calendar or a family calendar.

6. **Syncing with Devices:** For seamless access across various devices, consider syncing your Google Calendar with your smartphone, tablet, or other digital platforms. This ensures that your schedule is always at your fingertips, whether you're at your desk or on the go.

7. **Exploring Additional Settings:** Delve into the settings menu to explore additional customization options. Adjust notification preferences, event defaults, and sharing settings to fine-tune your Google Calendar experience.

8. **Personalizing Event Details:** Familiarize yourself with the process of adding events to your calendar. Provide detailed

information such as event titles, locations, and descriptions. Experiment with event reminders to suit your preferences for timely notifications.

By diligently following these steps, you lay the foundation for an organized and efficient scheduling experience with Google Calendar. Your personalized account setup ensures that the platform aligns seamlessly with your individual preferences and lifestyle, setting the stage for effective time management.

- **Navigating the Interface**

Effortless navigation lies at the heart of the Google Calendar experience, allowing users to seamlessly interact with their schedules. Familiarizing yourself with the interface ensures that you can effortlessly explore, manage, and optimize your calendar. Here's an overview of key elements within the Google Calendar interface:

1. **Main Calendar View:** Upon entering Google Calendar, you'll find the main calendar view. This provides an overview of your scheduled events, displayed in a daily, weekly, or monthly format. Toggle between these views based on your preferred level of detail.

2. **Date Navigation:** Easily traverse through dates using the navigation options. Navigate forward and backward through days,

weeks, or months to quickly locate specific events or plan for the future.

3. **Create Event Button:** Initiate event creation with a single click. The "+ Create" button, prominently positioned, allows you to swiftly add new events to your calendar. This streamlined process ensures that scheduling commitments is a hassle-free task.

4. **Search Bar:** Locate specific events efficiently using the search bar. Simply enter keywords, event titles, or participant names to quickly find relevant entries within your calendar.

5. **Side Navigation Panel:** The side navigation panel on the left provides quick access to various calendar views, including My Calendars, Other Calendars, and Tasks. This panel also houses options for creating reminders, exploring additional calendars, and accessing settings.

6. **Today Button:** Instantly return to the current date by clicking the "Today" button. This feature is particularly useful when navigating through future dates and want to swiftly return to the present.

7. **Event Details Popup:** Clicking on an event opens a detailed event details popup. This window displays comprehensive information about the selected event, including the title, time, location, and any additional details you've added during the event creation process.

8. **Calendar Settings:** Access the settings menu to personalize your Google Calendar experience. Here, you can fine-tune various preferences, adjust notification settings, and explore additional customization options.

9. **Quick Add Feature:** Expedite event creation with the Quick Add feature. Simply click on the "+" button, type your event details in natural language (e.g., "Meeting with John at 2 pm tomorrow"), and let Google Calendar interpret and schedule the event accordingly.

10. **Event Color Coding:** Enhance visual organization through color-coding. Each calendar can be assigned a distinct color, making it easy to differentiate between personal, work, and other commitments at a glance.

Mastering the art of navigating the Google Calendar interface empowers you to efficiently manage your schedule. Whether you're planning for the day, week, or month, the intuitive design ensures that you can effortlessly interact with your calendar, making time management a seamless and enjoyable process.

- **Customizing Calendar Settings**

Tailoring your Google Calendar to suit your preferences and needs is a key step in optimizing your scheduling experience. The platform offers a range of customizable settings that allow you to personalize everything from visual appearance to notification preferences. Here's a comprehensive guide to customizing your Google Calendar settings:

1. **Accessing Settings:** Begin by accessing the settings menu. Located in the side navigation panel, click on the gear icon labeled "Settings" to enter the customization hub.

2. **General Settings:** Explore the general settings to configure fundamental aspects of your calendar. Set your preferred language, adjust your default view (day, week, month), and specify the starting day of the week based on your regional or personal preferences.

3. **Event Settings:** Fine-tune your event-related preferences. Determine the default event duration, set your preferred event color scheme, and choose whether events should automatically be declined if they conflict with existing commitments.

4. **Notifications:** Manage your notification preferences to stay informed about upcoming events. Customize the timing and delivery method of notifications for various events, ensuring that you receive timely reminders that align with your workflow.

5. **View Options:** Personalize your calendar's appearance by experimenting with different view options. Choose between a classic or compact layout, adjust the density of event display, and explore other visual customization features.

6. **Working Hours:** Define your working hours to establish a clear distinction between professional commitments and personal

time. This feature helps in avoiding scheduling conflicts and ensures that your calendar aligns with your daily routine.

7. **Time Zone Settings:** If you frequently travel or collaborate with individuals in different time zones, accurately set your time zone preferences. This ensures that events are displayed and scheduled correctly, regardless of your geographical location.

8. **Weather Calendar Integration (Optional):** If staying updated on weather conditions is crucial for your planning, consider integrating a weather calendar. This provides real-time weather information directly within your Google Calendar interface.

9. **Other Calendars:** Manage additional calendars seamlessly. Explore options to add, edit, or remove calendars. Adjust sharing settings and permissions for a collaborative experience with colleagues, friends, or family.

10. **Mobile Setup:** Sync your Google Calendar with your mobile device for on-the-go access. The mobile setup section provides step-by-step instructions for integrating your calendar with smartphones or tablets.

11. **Lab Features (Optional):** For advanced users seeking additional functionalities, delve into the Labs section. Here, you can experiment with experimental features that enhance your calendar experience, although these features may still be in development.

By delving into these customizable settings, you shape your Google Calendar to align precisely with your preferences and requirements. This tailored approach transforms the platform into a personalized productivity hub, enhancing your ability to manage time effectively and stay organized in the digital landscape.

CHAPTER 2

CREATING AND MANAGING EVENTS

- **Adding Events to Your Calendar**

Efficiently adding events to your Google Calendar is a fundamental skill that empowers you to stay organized and on top of your schedule. The platform provides a user-friendly interface, making the event creation process straightforward. Here's a step-by-step guide to seamlessly add events to your Google Calendar:

1. **Navigate to Your Calendar:** Start by opening Google Calendar and ensuring you are in the main calendar view. If not, click on the appropriate date or switch to the desired view (day, week, month) where you want to add the event.

2. **Click on the Desired Date and Time:** Locate the date and time for your event within the calendar view. Click on the specific time slot or day where you want the event to occur.

3. **Create Event Popup:** A popup will appear, prompting you to create a new event. Here, enter the essential details:

- **Event Title:** Clearly specify the name of the event.

- **Event Date and Time:** Set the date and time for the event. Adjust the start and end times accordingly.

- **Location:** Add the venue or location for the event.

- **Description:** Include any additional information or context for the event.

4. **Additional Event Options:** Explore additional options within the popup to enhance your event:

- **Recurring Events:** If the event repeats, choose the recurrence pattern (daily, weekly, monthly).
- **Reminders:** Set reminders to receive notifications before the event starts.
- **Color Coding:** Assign a specific color to the event for visual organization.

5. **Save the Event:** Once you've entered the relevant details, click the "Save" button. Your event is now added to the calendar and will be visible in the specified date and time slot.

6. **Quick Add Feature (Optional):** For a swift event creation process, use the Quick Add feature. Click on the "+" button, type the event details in natural language (e.g., "Meeting with John at 2 pm tomorrow"), and let Google Calendar interpret and schedule the event.

7. **Edit or Delete Events:** If you need to make changes to an existing event, click on the event in the calendar view. The detailed event popup allows you to edit or delete the event as needed.

8. **Drag and Drop (Optional):** In some calendar views, you can also use the drag-and-drop feature to reschedule events. Click and hold on an event, then move it to the desired date and time.

By mastering the process of adding events to your Google Calendar, you harness the full potential of the platform for efficient time management. This foundational skill ensures that your schedule remains organized, accessible, and aligned with your commitments, whether they are professional meetings, personal appointments, or social gatherings.

- **Setting Event Details (Time, Location, Description)**

The effectiveness of your schedule relies heavily on the accuracy and clarity of event details. Google Calendar simplifies this process by providing a straightforward interface to set crucial event parameters. Here's a guide on how to precisely configure time, location, and description details for your events:

1. **Navigate to Your Calendar:**

- Open Google Calendar and ensure you are in the main calendar view.

- Select the date and time slot for the event you want to detail.

2. **Create Event Popup:**

- Click on the chosen date and time to open the event creation popup.

3. **Event Title:**

- Clearly articulate the name of your event in the "Event title" field.

4. **Event Date and Time:**

- Set the date and time for your event using the respective fields.
- Adjust the start and end times to accurately reflect the duration of the event.

5. **Location:**

- Specify the venue or location of the event in the "Location" field.
- Google Calendar integrates with Google Maps for seamless location identification.

6. **Description:**

- Enhance event clarity by providing additional context or information in the "Description" field.
- Include relevant details such as agenda items, discussion points, or any preparations needed.

7. **Recurring Events (Optional):**

- If the event is recurring, explore the recurring event options.
- Choose the recurrence pattern (daily, weekly, monthly) to streamline repetitive scheduling.

8. **Reminders:**

- Set reminders to receive timely notifications before the event starts.
- Customizable reminder options ensure you stay prepared and punctual.

9. **Color Coding (Optional):**

- Assign a specific color to the event to visually categorize it within your calendar.
- Color coding aids in quick differentiation between various types of events.

10. **Save the Event:**

- Once all details are entered, click the "Save" button to confirm and save your event.
- The event will now appear in your calendar with the specified details.

11. **Edit or Delete Events:**

- If changes are necessary, click on the event in the calendar view to access the detailed event popup.
- Edit or delete the event as needed to keep your calendar accurate.

12. **Quick Add Feature (Optional):**

- Alternatively, utilize the Quick Add feature for expedited event creation.
- Type event details in natural language (e.g., "Meeting with John at 2 pm tomorrow") and let Google Calendar interpret and schedule the event.

By meticulously setting event details in Google Calendar, you ensure that your schedule is comprehensive and well-defined. Accurate information regarding time, location, and descriptions enhances your ability to manage commitments effectively, fostering a streamlined and organized approach to time management.

- **Recurring Events and Reminders**

Google Calendar's flexibility extends to handling recurring events, providing a convenient way to schedule repetitive commitments. Additionally, the platform empowers users with customizable reminders, ensuring timely notifications for upcoming events. Here's how to effectively manage recurring events and reminders in Google Calendar:

Recurring Events:

1. **Navigate to Your Calendar:**

- Open Google Calendar and select the date and time slot for the recurring event.

2. **Create Event Popup:**

- Click on the chosen date and time to open the event creation popup.

3. **Event Title:**

- Clearly define the event's name in the "Event title" field.

4. **Event Date and Time:**

- Set the initial date and time for the event using the respective fields.

5. **Recurring Event Options:**

- Explore the recurring event options within the popup.
- Choose the recurrence pattern (daily, weekly, monthly) that aligns with the event's frequency.

6. **Custom Recurrence:**

- For more complex recurrence patterns, utilize the "Custom" option to tailor the schedule precisely.

7. **End Repeat:**

- Specify an end date for the recurring series, ensuring the events conclude when needed.

8. **Save the Recurring Event:**

- Click the "Save" button to confirm and save the recurring event.
- The series of events will now populate your calendar based on the specified recurrence.

9. **Edit or Delete Recurring Events:**

- To make adjustments, click on any event within the series to access the detailed popup.
- Edit or delete the series as needed, with the option to apply changes to future occurrences.

Reminders:

1. **Set Reminders During Event Creation:**

- While creating an event, navigate to the "Reminders" section in the event popup.

2. **Customize Reminder Timing:**

- Set reminders for specific times before the event starts, ensuring you receive timely notifications.
- Customize reminder preferences based on your preferences and workflow.

3. **Multiple Reminders:**

- Add multiple reminders for a single event, providing flexibility in managing your schedule.

4. **Default Reminders:**

- Configure default reminder settings in the general settings menu for consistent application across all events.

5. **Receive Notifications:**

- Ensure that notifications are enabled on your device to receive reminders promptly.

6. **View and Manage Reminders:**

- View and manage reminders for all your events in the "Reminders" section of the side navigation panel.

7. **Adjust Reminders as Needed:**

- Click on an event to access the detailed popup and make adjustments to reminders as your schedule evolves.

By adeptly managing recurring events and reminders in Google Calendar, you harness the platform's capabilities to streamline repetitive scheduling and stay informed about upcoming commitments. This proactive approach to scheduling contributes to effective time management and ensures that you never miss a crucial event.

- **Color Coding for Organization**

Google Calendar's color-coding feature is a powerful organizational tool that allows you to visually categorize and differentiate between various types of events at a glance. Implementing a thoughtful color-coding system enhances your ability to quickly interpret your schedule and prioritize tasks. Here's how to effectively use color coding in Google Calendar:

1. **Navigate to Your Calendar:**

- Open Google Calendar and ensure you are in the main calendar view.

2. **Create or Select an Event:**

- Either create a new event or select an existing one that you want to color-code.

3. **Choose a Color:**

- In the event creation or editing popup, locate the "Event color" option.

- Click on the color palette icon to reveal a spectrum of colors.

4. **Select a Meaningful Color:**

- Choose a color that corresponds to the type or category of the event.
- For example, use red for work-related events, blue for personal commitments, and green for social activities.

5. **Save the Event:**

- After selecting the color, save the event. The chosen color will now be associated with that particular event.

6. **Consistent Color Coding:**

- Establish a consistent color-coding system across your calendar. Assign the same color to events of a similar nature for clarity.

7. **Multiple Calendars, Multiple Colors:**

- If you are using multiple calendars, each calendar can have its unique set of colors. This further refines organization, especially if you have separate calendars for work, personal, or other categories.

8. **Quick Identification:**

- As you scroll through your calendar, the color-coded events stand out, making it easy to identify and focus on specific types of activities.

9. **Edit or Update Colors:**

- To edit or update the color of an event, click on the event, access the detailed popup, and adjust the color as needed.

10. **Color Coding Best Practices:**

- Opt for a limited color palette to avoid visual clutter.
- Consider creating a legend or key to remind yourself of the meaning behind each color.
- Use bright or bold colors for high-priority or important events.

11. **Mobile Accessibility:**

- Colors applied to events on the desktop version of Google Calendar will also reflect on the mobile app, providing a consistent organizational system across devices.

By incorporating color coding into your Google Calendar, you transform it into a visual roadmap that instantly communicates the nature and importance of your commitments. This intuitive organizational strategy enhances your ability to manage time effectively and fosters a clear understanding of your schedule.

- **Managing and Editing Events**

Efficiently managing and editing events in Google Calendar ensures that your schedule remains dynamic and reflects the evolving nature of your commitments. Whether adapting to changes or refining event details, the platform provides intuitive tools for effective event management. Here's a guide on how to navigate the process seamlessly:

Managing Events:

1. **Navigate to Your Calendar:**

- Open Google Calendar and locate the event you want to manage.

2. **View Options:**

- Adjust the calendar view to focus on the desired timeframe, making it easier to locate the event.

3. **Click on the Event:**

- Click on the event in the calendar view to access the detailed event popup.

4. **View and Modify Details:**

- Review event details such as title, date, time, location, and description within the popup.
- Modify any details as needed.

5. **Event Actions:**

- Utilize the event actions menu within the popup to perform common tasks, such as copying the event, duplicating it, or deleting it.

6. **Drag-and-Drop (Optional):**

- In certain calendar views, you can drag and drop events to reschedule them effortlessly.

7. **Managing Recurring Events:**

- For recurring events, choose whether changes apply to a single instance or the entire series.

8. **Save Changes:**

- After making adjustments, click the "Save" button to confirm the changes.

Editing Events:

1. **Navigate to Your Calendar:**

- Open Google Calendar and locate the event you want to edit.

2. **View Options:**

- Adjust the calendar view to focus on the desired timeframe, making it easier to locate the event.

3. **Click on the Event:**

- Click on the event in the calendar view to access the detailed event popup.

4. **Edit Event Details:**

- Modify event details such as title, date, time, location, and description within the popup.

5. **Recurring Event Edits:**

- For recurring events, choose whether changes apply to a single instance or the entire series.

6. **Customizing Reminders:**

- Adjust reminder settings or add new reminders based on your preferences.

7. **Changing Color:**

- Modify the color of the event for visual organization if needed.

8. **Save Changes:**

- After editing, click the "Save" button to confirm the changes.

9. **Undo Changes (Optional):**

- If you accidentally make changes, use the "Undo" button to revert to the previous state.

10. **Delete Event (Optional):**

- If you decide to remove the event entirely, use the delete option within the event actions menu.

11. **Mobile Editing:**

- Changes made on the desktop version of Google Calendar will sync with the mobile app for a seamless experience.

By mastering the art of managing and editing events in Google Calendar, you ensure that your schedule remains agile and aligned with your current priorities. This proactive approach to event management contributes to effective time management and enables you to adapt to changes effortlessly.

CHAPTER 3
MASTERING CALENDAR VIEWS

- **Daily, Weekly, Monthly Views**

Google Calendar offers a versatile interface with multiple viewing options, allowing you to tailor your experience based on your scheduling preferences. Whether you prefer a detailed daily overview, a broader weekly perspective, or a comprehensive monthly layout, mastering these views enhances your ability to manage your time effectively. Here's a guide on how to navigate daily, weekly, and monthly views in Google Calendar:

Daily View:

1. **Navigate to Your Calendar:**

- Open Google Calendar and ensure you are in the main calendar view.

2. **Select the Daily View:**

- Click on the "Day" view option, usually represented as a single square on the calendar view.

3. **Review Your Day:**

- The daily view provides a detailed breakdown of your schedule for the selected day.

- Easily navigate through hours and minutes to review events and commitments.

4. **Create or Edit Events:**

- Add new events or edit existing ones directly within the daily view for precise scheduling.

5. **Scroll Through Time:**

- If your day extends beyond the visible hours, scroll through the timeline to view later parts of the day.

Weekly View:

1. **Navigate to Your Calendar:**

- Open Google Calendar and ensure you are in the main calendar view.

2. **Select the Weekly View:**

- Click on the "Week" view option, typically represented as a set of seven squares, one for each day of the week.

3. **Review Your Week:**

- The weekly view provides a condensed overview of your schedule for the entire week.
- Each day is segmented horizontally, making it easy to identify daily commitments.

4. **Create or Edit Events:**

- Add or edit events directly within the weekly view, offering a comprehensive outlook of your week.

5. **Navigate Between Weeks:**

- Scroll through weeks to plan or review events beyond the current week.

Monthly View:

1. **Navigate to Your Calendar:**

- Open Google Calendar and ensure you are in the main calendar view.

2. **Select the Monthly View:**

- Click on the "Month" view option, usually represented as a grid with each square corresponding to a day.

3. **Review Your Month:**

- The monthly view provides a bird's-eye view of your schedule for the entire month.
- Each day is represented by a square, and events are displayed within their respective date boxes.

4. **Create or Edit Events:**

- While the monthly view offers a broader perspective, you can still add or edit events directly within the date boxes.

5. **Navigate Between Months:**

- Scroll through months to plan or review events beyond the current month.

6. **Detailed Event Information (Optional):**

- Hover over an event in the monthly view to view basic details. Clicking on the event provides more detailed information and editing options.

By seamlessly navigating through daily, weekly, and monthly views in Google Calendar, you tailor your scheduling experience to align with your preferred level of detail and planning horizon. This flexibility ensures that you can effectively manage your time, whether focusing on the intricacies of a single day or gaining a broader perspective for the entire month.

- **Custom Views and Filters**

Google Calendar provides a robust set of features for customizing your scheduling experience, allowing you to create personalized views and filters to cater to your specific needs. By harnessing these tools, you can streamline your calendar interface, focus on key aspects of your schedule, and enhance overall efficiency. Here's a guide on how to create custom views and filters in Google Calendar:

Custom Views:

1. **Navigate to Your Calendar:**

- Open Google Calendar and ensure you are in the main calendar view.

2. **Access View Options:**

- Look for the view options, usually located in the top-right corner.
- Common view options include "Day," "Week," "Month," and "Agenda."

3. **Customize Time Range:**

- Some calendar views allow you to customize the time range displayed. Use this feature to focus on specific periods, such as mornings or afternoons.

4. **Create Additional Calendars (Optional):**

- If you have multiple calendars for different purposes (e.g., work, personal), consider creating additional calendars to maintain a clear separation.

5. **Overlay Calendars (Optional):**

- Use the "Overlay" feature to overlay multiple calendars, providing a consolidated view of events from different calendars.

6. **Color-Coding for Visual Organization:**

- Leverage color-coding to visually distinguish events based on categories or priorities within your custom view.

7. **Save Custom View Settings:**

- Once you've configured your preferred settings, check if your calendar platform allows you to save custom views. This ensures easy access to your personalized layouts.

Custom Filters:

1. **Navigate to Your Calendar:**

- Open Google Calendar and ensure you are in the main calendar view.

2. **Access Filter Options:**

- Look for the filter options, typically located in the side navigation panel.

3. **Create New Filter:**

- Explore the option to create a new filter. This might involve specifying criteria such as event types, calendars, or keywords.

4. **Define Filter Parameters:**

- Specify the parameters for your filter. This could include filtering by specific calendars, event titles, or keywords.

5. **Save the Filter:**

- Once you've defined your filter, save it for future use. Some calendar platforms allow you to name your filters for easy identification.

6. **Apply Filters:**

- Apply your custom filters to streamline your calendar view. This narrows down the displayed events to those meeting your specified criteria.

7. **Toggle Between Filters:**

- If your calendar platform supports it, create multiple filters for different scenarios. Toggle between filters based on your current focus or needs.

8. **Review and Adjust Filtered Views:**

- Regularly review your filtered views and adjust filter parameters as your scheduling priorities evolve.

By mastering custom views and filters in Google Calendar, you tailor the platform to suit your unique preferences and workflow. This customization not only enhances the clarity of your schedule but also allows you to focus on the events that matter most at any given time.

- **Utilizing the Agenda View**

The Agenda view in Google Calendar serves as a dynamic tool for individuals who prefer a chronological and detailed overview of their upcoming events and commitments. By effectively utilizing this feature, you can enhance your ability to plan, prioritize, and stay organized. Here's a guide on how to make the most of the Agenda view in Google Calendar:

1. **Navigate to Your Calendar:**

- Open Google Calendar and ensure you are in the main calendar view.

2. **Access Agenda View:**

- Locate and click on the "Agenda" view option. This view is designed to provide a list of your upcoming events in chronological order.

3. **Review Daily Schedule:**

- The Agenda view offers a day-by-day breakdown of your schedule, making it easy to review your commitments at a glance.

4. **Scroll Through Dates:**

- Navigate forward and backward through dates to review past and future events. The Agenda view is particularly useful for planning your day or week.

5. **Detailed Event Information:**

- Each event in the Agenda view displays detailed information, including the event title, time, and location. This level of detail ensures clarity and helps you stay prepared.

6. **Interactive Event Links:**

- Click on an event in the Agenda view to access additional details. Some calendar platforms allow you to interact directly with event links or attachments.

7. **Custom Time Range:**

- Customize the time range displayed in the Agenda view to focus on specific hours or a broader timeframe based on your preferences.

8. **Search and Filter Events:**

- Use the search bar or filtering options within the Agenda view to locate specific events or types of commitments quickly.

9. **Multi-Calendar Support:**

- If you have multiple calendars, the Agenda view consolidates events from all calendars, providing a unified and comprehensive schedule.

10. **Add Events on the Fly:**

- While in the Agenda view, easily add new events directly from the list by selecting the appropriate time slot.

11. **Mobile Accessibility:**

- Access the Agenda view seamlessly on your mobile device, ensuring that you can stay organized even when on the go.

12. **Printable Agenda (Optional):**

- Some calendar platforms offer the option to print your Agenda view. This can be useful for creating physical copies of your schedule for reference.

13. **Export Agenda (Optional):**

- Explore options to export your Agenda view for sharing or integrating it with other productivity tools.

By embracing the Agenda view in Google Calendar, you transform your scheduling experience into a detailed and organized plan. This chronological overview empowers you to stay on top of your commitments, prioritize tasks effectively, and make informed decisions about your time management.

- **Integrating Multiple Calendars**

Integrating multiple calendars within Google Calendar enł your ability to manage various aspects of your life, whether it's work, personal commitments, or shared schedules. By consolidating multiple calendars into one cohesive interface, you streamline your scheduling experience. Here's a comprehensive guide on how to seamlessly integrate and manage multiple calendars in Google Calendar:

1. **Access Google Calendar:**

- Open Google Calendar and ensure you are in the main calendar view.

2. **Locate "My Calendars" Section:**

- Look for the "My Calendars" section in the side navigation panel. This section displays the calendars associated with your Google Account.

3. **Add Additional Calendars:**

- Click on "Add Calendar" to add additional calendars to your account. You can add calendars created by you or shared calendars from other users.

4. **Create a New Calendar:**

- If needed, create a new calendar by clicking on "Create new calendar" in the "My Calendars" section. This is particularly useful for categorizing events based on different aspects of your life.

5. **Color Code Calendars:**

- Assign distinct colors to each calendar to visually differentiate them. This color-coding strategy enhances clarity when viewing events from multiple calendars.

6. **Toggle Visibility of Calendars:**

- Use the checkboxes next to each calendar name to toggle the visibility of specific calendars. This feature allows you to focus on relevant schedules and declutter your view.

7. **Overlay Calendars (Optional):**

- Experiment with the "Overlay" feature, allowing you to overlay multiple calendars in the same view. This consolidated view provides a comprehensive overview of all selected calendars.

8. **Manage Calendar Settings:**

- Click on the settings icon next to each calendar in the "My Calendars" section to access specific calendar settings. Here, you can adjust sharing settings, customize color preferences, and manage notifications.

9. **View Aggregated Schedule:**

- In the main calendar view, toggle between different calendars to view an aggregated schedule. This consolidated view includes events from all selected calendars.

10. **Sync Calendars Across Devices:**

- Ensure that calendar synchronization is enabled across your devices. This ensures that any changes or additions made on one device reflect on all devices seamlessly.

11. **Sharing Calendars (Optional):**

- Share specific calendars with others if you collaborate on events or need to coordinate schedules. Adjust sharing settings based on the level of access you want to provide.

12. **Import External Calendars (Optional):**

- Explore options to import external calendars, such as public holidays or sports schedules, to enhance the comprehensiveness of your calendar.

13. **Quickly Add Events to Specific Calendars:**

- When creating a new event, choose the calendar where you want to add the event. This ensures that the event is categorized appropriately.

14. **Remove Calendars (Optional):**

- If you no longer need a particular calendar, you can remove it from your account. Be cautious, as this action deletes all events associated with that calendar.

By masterfully integrating multiple calendars in Google Calendar, you create a centralized hub for your scheduling needs. This streamlined approach allows you to efficiently manage diverse commitments, ensuring that you stay organized and on top of your various responsibilities.

- **Syncing with External Calendars and Devices**

Syncing Google Calendar with external calendars and devices is a key strategy to ensure that your schedule remains up-to-date across platforms. This seamless integration enhances accessibility and enables you to manage your commitments efficiently. Here's a comprehensive guide on how to effortlessly sync Google Calendar with external calendars and devices:

Syncing with External Calendars:

1. **Navigate to Your Calendar:**

- Open Google Calendar and ensure you are in the main calendar view.

2. **Access "Settings":**

- Click on the settings icon, often represented as a gear, to access the settings menu.

3. **Select "Settings" (or "View All Settings" on some platforms):**

- Navigate to the "Settings" menu. This may be labeled differently on various platforms.

4. **Choose "Calendars":**

- Within the settings menu, select "Calendars" to manage your calendar configurations.

5. **Click on the Specific Calendar:**

- Identify the calendar you want to sync with an external calendar and click on it.

6. **Scroll Down to "Integrate Calendar":**

- Scroll down to find the "Integrate Calendar" or "Integrate with other calendars" section.

7. **Select External Calendar Integration:**

- Choose the type of external calendar you want to sync with (e.g., Outlook, Apple Calendar, or any supported calendar application).

8. **Follow On-Screen Instructions:**

- Follow the on-screen instructions to complete the integration process. This typically involves providing necessary permissions and authentication.

9. **Review Sync Settings:**

- After integration, review the sync settings to ensure that the frequency and details of the sync meet your preferences.

10. **Repeat for Multiple Calendars (Optional):**

- If you have multiple calendars, repeat the process for each calendar you want to sync with an external calendar.

Syncing with Devices:

1. **Access Google Calendar on Devices:**

- Ensure that you have the Google Calendar app installed on your mobile devices.

2. **Sign in to Your Google Account:**

- Sign in to the Google Account associated with your Google Calendar.

3. **Enable Calendar Sync:**

- In the app settings, enable calendar sync to ensure that your Google Calendar events are accessible on your device.

4. **Adjust Sync Settings (Optional):**

- Explore the sync settings on your device to customize how and when calendar events are updated.

5. **Sync with Apple Devices (Optional):**

- On Apple devices, such as iPhones and iPads, ensure that your Google Calendar is added to the Apple Calendar app for seamless integration.

6. **Sync with Other Calendar Apps (Optional):**

- If you use third-party calendar apps, ensure that they are configured to sync with your Google Calendar. Follow the app-specific instructions for integration.

7. **Syncing with Desktop Calendars:**

- On desktops, use the Google Calendar web version or integrate it with desktop calendar applications to ensure synchronization.

8. **Verify Sync Across Devices:**

- Test the sync by adding or modifying events on one device and confirming that changes reflect on other synced devices.

9. **Review Notifications and Alerts:**

- Confirm that notifications and alerts for events are synchronized across all your devices for timely reminders.

10. **Troubleshoot Sync Issues (If Necessary):**

- If you encounter sync issues, review the settings on both Google Calendar and your devices. Ensure that permissions are granted, and troubleshoot any connectivity issues.

By following these steps, you establish a seamless connection between Google Calendar, external calendars, and your devices. This synchronization ensures that your schedule is accessible and consistent across different platforms, empowering you to stay organized and on top of your commitments.

CHAPTER 4

COLLABORATION AND SHARING

- **Inviting Others to Events**

Collaborative scheduling becomes a breeze in Google Calendar, thanks to its invitation features. By inviting others to your events, you streamline communication, ensure everyone is on the same page, and foster efficient coordination. Here's a step-by-step guide on how to invite others to your events in Google Calendar:

1. **Navigate to Your Calendar:**

- Open Google Calendar and ensure you are in the main calendar view.

2. **Create a New Event:**

- Click on the desired date and time to create a new event.

3. **Enter Event Details:**

- In the event creation popup, enter the event details such as title, date, time, location, and description.

4. **Access the "Add Guests" Section:**

- Look for the "Add guests" or "Guests" section in the event creation popup. This is where you'll invite others to the event.

5. **Enter Guest Email Addresses:**

- Enter the email addresses of the individuals you want to invite. Google Calendar will automatically suggest contacts from your Google Contacts.

6. **Set Permissions (Optional):**

- Choose the appropriate permission level for guests. Options may include "See only free/busy," "See all event details," or "Make changes to events."

7. **Send Invitations:**

- Click the "Save" or "Send" button to send invitations to the specified guests. They will receive email invitations with event details.

8. **Review Guest Responses:**

- Guests can respond to invitations, indicating whether they will attend, may attend, or cannot attend. Their responses are updated in real-time on your calendar.

9. **Edit or Remove Guests (Optional):**

- If needed, click on the event in your calendar view to access the event popup. From here, you can edit or remove guests.

10. **Automatic Updates for Changes:**

- Any changes you make to the event, such as adjusting the time or location, are automatically updated for invited guests.

11. **Send Updates (Optional):**

- If you make significant changes to the event, consider sending updates to guests. This ensures that they have the latest information.

12. **Receive Notifications (Guests):**

- Guests receive email notifications for event invitations, updates, and reminders. They can also view the event details directly in their own Google Calendar.

13. **Respond to Invitations (Guests):**

- Guests can respond to invitations directly from their email or through the Google Calendar interface, indicating their attendance status.

14. **Collaborate in Event Details (Optional):**

- Guests can collaborate within the event details by adding comments or attachments. This fosters communication and coordination leading up to the event.

By incorporating these steps into your event planning process, you transform Google Calendar into a collaborative hub. Inviting others to your events ensures that everyone involved is well-informed, and the coordination process is streamlined. This collaborative approach is particularly valuable for work meetings, social gatherings, and any events where effective communication is key.

- **Sharing Entire Calendars**

Sharing your entire calendar in Google Calendar is a powerful way to provide others with a comprehensive view of your schedule. Whether it's for work, family, or collaborative projects, sharing your calendar fosters transparency and facilitates effective coordination. Here's a detailed guide on how to share your entire calendar in Google Calendar:

1. **Navigate to Your Calendar:**

- Open Google Calendar and ensure you are in the main calendar view.

2. **Access "Settings":**

- Click on the settings icon, usually represented as a gear, to access the settings menu.

3. **Select "Settings" (or "View All Settings" on some platforms):**

- Navigate to the "Settings" menu. This may be labeled differently on various platforms.

4. **Choose "Calendars":**

- Within the settings menu, select "Calendars" to manage your calendar configurations.

5. **Locate Your Calendar:**

- Identify the calendar you want to share. Click on the calendar name to access specific calendar settings.

6. **Access "Share with Others":**

- Look for the "Share with others" or "Share this calendar" option. Click on it to begin the sharing process.

7. **Specify Sharing Settings:**

- Choose the level of access you want to grant to others. Options may include "See only free/busy," "See all event details," or "Make changes to events."

8. **Enter Email Addresses:**

- Enter the email addresses of the individuals you want to share your calendar with. You can separate multiple email addresses with commas.

9. **Set Permissions (Optional):**

- For each email address, set the appropriate permission level. This allows you to customize access for different individuals.

10. **Notify People (Optional):**

- Choose whether to notify the people you're sharing with via email. This email will contain a link to your shared calendar.

11. **Save or Send Invitations:**

- Click the "Save" or "Send" button to save your sharing settings and send invitations to the specified individuals.

12. **Review Shared Calendar:**

- Once shared, your calendar will appear in the "Other calendars" section of the invited individuals' Google Calendar. They can toggle it on or off as needed.

13. **Access "Access permissions" (Optional):**

- In some platforms, you may find an "Access permissions" section where you can review and modify the access settings for individuals.

14. **Modify or Remove Sharing (Optional):**

- If you need to modify or remove sharing, return to the calendar settings and adjust the sharing options accordingly.

15. **Shared Calendar Updates:**

- Any changes you make to your calendar, including new events or modifications, are automatically updated for those with whom you've shared the calendar.

16. **Receive Notifications (Shared Individuals):**

- Individuals with access to your shared calendar will receive notifications for events based on the permissions you've granted.

By following these steps, you establish a transparent and collaborative environment by sharing your entire calendar in Google Calendar. This level of access allows others to view and, if permitted, interact with your schedule, fostering effective communication and coordination.

- **Managing Permissions**

Managing permissions in Google Calendar is essential for controlling who can view, modify, or collaborate on your events. Fine-tuning these settings ensures that your scheduling information remains secure and that collaboration is both efficient and controlled. Here's a comprehensive guide on how to master permissions in Google Calendar:

Managing Calendar Permissions:

1. **Navigate to Your Calendar:**

- Open Google Calendar and ensure you are in the main calendar view.

2. **Access "Settings":**

- Click on the settings icon, usually represented as a gear, to access the settings menu.

3. **Select "Settings" (or "View All Settings" on some platforms):**

- Navigate to the "Settings" menu. This may be labeled differently on various platforms.

4. **Choose "Calendars":**

- Within the settings menu, select "Calendars" to manage your calendar configurations.

5. **Locate Your Calendar:**

- Identify the calendar for which you want to manage permissions. Click on the calendar name to access specific calendar settings.

6. **Access "Share with Others":**

- Look for the "Share with others" or "Share this calendar" option. Click on it to view and manage existing permissions.

7. **Review Existing Permissions:**

- A list of individuals or groups with whom you've shared your calendar will be displayed. Review the current permissions for each entry.

8. **Modify Permissions:**

- To modify permissions, click on the name or email address of the individual or group. Adjust the permission level as needed. Options may include "See only free/busy," "See all event details," or "Make changes to events."

9. **Add New Individuals (Optional):**

- If you want to add new individuals to share your calendar with, click the "+ Add people" button. Enter their email addresses and set the appropriate permissions.

10. **Notify People (Optional):**

- Choose whether to notify the people you're sharing with via email. This email will contain a link to your shared calendar.

11. **Remove Permissions:**

- To remove permissions, click on the name or email address of the individual or group and select "Remove" or adjust the permission level to "See only free/busy."

12. **Access "Access permissions" (Optional):**

- Some platforms provide an "Access permissions" section where you can review and modify the access settings for individuals.

13. **Review Shared Calendar:**

- Once you've adjusted permissions, review your shared calendar to ensure that only the intended individuals have the appropriate level of access.

Managing Event Permissions:

1. **Create or Edit an Event:**

- Click on a date and time to create a new event or click on an existing event to edit it.

2. **Access Guest Permissions:**

- In the event creation or editing popup, locate the "Add guests" or "Guests" section.

3. **Specify Guest Permissions:**

- For each guest, set the appropriate permission level. This allows you to customize access for different individuals. Options may include "See only free/busy," "See all event details," or "Make changes to events."

4. **Send Invitations:**

- Click the "Save" or "Send" button to send invitations to the specified guests. They will receive email invitations with event details.

5. **Review Guest Responses:**

- Guests can respond to invitations, indicating whether they will attend, may attend, or cannot attend. Their responses are updated in real-time on your calendar.

6. **Modify or Remove Guests (Optional):**

- If needed, click on the event in your calendar view to access the event popup. From here, you can edit or remove guests.

7. **Review Shared Event Details:**

- Ensure that guests have the appropriate level of access to event details based on the permissions you've set.

By mastering these steps, you gain control over who can access and interact with your calendar and individual events. This level of granularity in managing permissions ensures that your scheduling information is shared securely and that collaboration is tailored to your specific needs.

- **Collaborative Scheduling Tools**

Google Calendar offers a plethora of collaborative features and tools that facilitate seamless scheduling and coordination. Leveraging these tools enhances teamwork, ensures everyone is on the same page, and streamlines the planning process. Here's a guide on the collaborative scheduling tools available in Google Calendar:

1. Shared Calendars:

- *What it does:* Allows you to share entire calendars with individuals or groups.

- *How to use:* Access calendar settings, choose "Share with others," enter email addresses, and set permission levels.

2. Event Invitations:

- *What it does:* Enables you to invite others to specific events, controlling access and collaboration.

- *How to use:* When creating or editing an event, enter guest email addresses, set permissions, and send invitations.

3. Guest Notifications:

- *What it does:* Sends email notifications to guests for event invitations, updates, and reminders.
- *How to use:* Ensure that the "Notify people" option is selected when sending invitations.

4. Real-Time Updates:

- *What it does:* Keeps all collaborators updated with real-time changes to shared calendars and events.
- *How to use:* Any modifications to calendars or events are automatically reflected for all collaborators.

5. Event Comments:

- *What it does:* Facilitates communication and collaboration by allowing guests to add comments to specific events.
- *How to use:* Guests can add comments within the event details, fostering discussion and coordination.

6. Multiple Calendars:

- *What it does:* Enables the creation of multiple calendars for different aspects of life or projects.

- *How to use:* Create additional calendars and customize sharing settings for each.

7. Overlay Calendars:

- *What it does:* Provides a consolidated view by overlaying multiple calendars in the same interface.
- *How to use:* Access the calendar settings and experiment with the "Overlay" feature.

8. Calendar Permissions:

- *What it does:* Allows you to fine-tune who can view, edit, or collaborate on your calendar.
- *How to use:* Access calendar settings, choose "Share with others," and adjust permission levels.

9. Access Permissions:

- *What it does:* Provides detailed control over who can access specific calendars and their permission levels.
- *How to use:* Some platforms offer an "Access permissions" section in calendar settings for further customization.

10. Event Attachments: - *What it does:* Enables you to attach documents, files, or links to events for easy access. - *How to use:* When creating or editing an event, look for the attachment icon to add relevant files or links.

11. Event Reminders: - *What it does:* Sends reminders to collaborators before events, ensuring everyone is prepared. - *How to use:* Set reminder preferences when creating or editing an event.

12. Collaborative Mobile Access: - *What it does:* Provides seamless access to collaborative scheduling tools on mobile devices. - *How to use:* Download the Google Calendar app and sign in to your Google Account for on-the-go collaboration.

13. Integration with Google Meet: - *What it does:* Integrates seamlessly with Google Meet for scheduling and hosting virtual meetings. - *How to use:* When creating an event, choose "Add Google Meet video conferencing."

14. External Calendar Integration: - *What it does:* Allows syncing with external calendars (e.g., Outlook, Apple Calendar) for cross-platform collaboration. - *How to use:* Access calendar settings and follow the integration process for specific external calendars.

By incorporating these collaborative scheduling tools into your workflow, you optimize the efficiency of teamwork, ensure clear communication, and create a synchronized approach to managing schedules and events in Google Calendar.

- **Using Google Meet for Virtual Meetings**

Google Meet is an integrated video conferencing tool that seamlessly works with Google Calendar, making virtual meetings a breeze. Whether it's for work, team collaborations, or connecting with friends, Google Meet offers a robust platform for face-to-face interactions. Here's a guide on how to use Google Meet for virtual meetings in conjunction with Google Calendar:

1. Schedule a Meeting with Google Meet:

- When creating a new event in Google Calendar, click on "Add Google Meet video conferencing" to automatically generate a meeting link.

2. Join a Meeting:

- Access the meeting link directly from the event in Google Calendar at the scheduled time. Click "Join with Google Meet."

3. Start an Instant Meeting:

- If you need to host an impromptu meeting, click on the "+ New Meeting" button in the Google Meet interface or use the "Start Meeting" option in Google Calendar.

4. Invite Participants:

- When creating or editing an event in Google Calendar, add participants' email addresses. They will receive invitations with the Google Meet link.

5. Mobile Access:

- Download the Google Meet app on your mobile device for convenient access to virtual meetings on the go.

6. Screen Sharing:

- During a Google Meet session, use the screen sharing feature to present documents, slides, or any content on your screen.

7. Collaborative Editing with Google Workspace:

- Integrate Google Workspace tools like Google Docs, Sheets, and Slides for real-time collaborative editing during the meeting.

8. Recording Meetings:

- If allowed by the meeting organizer, record the Google Meet session for future reference. The recording is stored on Google Drive.

9. Chat Functionality:

- Use the chat feature within Google Meet to send messages, links, or important information to participants.

10. Manage Participants: - As the host, manage participant access by admitting or denying entry, muting participants, or removing individuals from the meeting.

11. Meeting Controls: - Familiarize yourself with meeting controls such as muting/unmuting, turning the camera on/off, and adjusting settings for optimal video and audio quality.

12. Calendar Integration: - Google Meet automatically integrates with Google Calendar, displaying upcoming meetings in your calendar view.

13. Integration with Google Chat: - Google Meet is seamlessly integrated with Google Chat, enhancing communication and collaboration within your team.

14. Share Meeting Links: - Share the Google Meet link directly from the event in Google Calendar or use the unique meeting code for easy access.

15. Customize Meeting Settings: - Explore and customize Google Meet settings, such as video quality, screen layout, and background blur, to enhance your virtual meeting experience.

16. End a Meeting: - As the host, end the meeting when it concludes. Participants will be automatically disconnected, and the meeting link becomes inactive.

By incorporating these tips into your virtual meeting routine, you leverage the full potential of Google Meet for effective and collaborative remote interactions. The seamless integration with Google Calendar enhances scheduling and ensures a streamlined experience for both hosts and participants.

CHAPTER 5

INTEGRATING TASKS AND TO-DO LISTS

- **Creating Tasks in Google Calendar**

Google Calendar seamlessly integrates task management features, providing a comprehensive platform for organizing your schedule and to-do lists. Here's a guide on how to create tasks in Google Calendar for efficient and centralized task management:

1. Open Google Calendar:

- Ensure you are logged into your Google Account and open Google Calendar.

2. Access "Tasks" View:

- Locate the "Tasks" view in the side panel. If it's not visible, click on the "Tasks" icon to reveal the tasks view.

3. Create a New Task:

- Click on the "+ New task" button within the "Tasks" view to create a new task.

4. Enter Task Details:

- In the task creation popup, enter details such as the task title, due date, and any additional notes or descriptions.

5. Set Due Dates and Times:

- Specify a due date and time for the task, if applicable. This helps prioritize tasks based on deadlines.

6. Add Subtasks (Optional):

- If your task involves multiple steps, consider adding subtasks to break down the larger task into more manageable components.

7. Assign Tasks to Lists (Optional):

- Organize your tasks by assigning them to specific lists or categories. This can be helpful for differentiating work, personal, or project-related tasks.

8. Drag and Drop Tasks:

- In the "Tasks" view, you can easily rearrange tasks by dragging and dropping them to adjust their order.

9. Mark Tasks as Complete:

- Once a task is completed, click the checkbox next to the task to mark it as done. The task will be visually crossed out.

10. View Tasks in Calendar (Optional): - Toggle the visibility of tasks in the main calendar view by clicking on the checkbox next to "Tasks" in the side panel.

11. View Tasks on Mobile Devices: - Access and manage your tasks on the go by using the Google Calendar app on your mobile device.

12. Set Reminders for Tasks: - Enhance task management by setting reminders for important tasks. Receive notifications to stay on top of your to-do list.

13. Sync Tasks Across Devices: - Ensure that task synchronization is enabled across your devices, allowing you to access and update tasks seamlessly.

14. Customize Task Colors (Optional): - Some platforms allow you to customize the colors of tasks for visual organization. Assign distinct colors to different types of tasks.

15. Export Tasks (Optional): - Explore options to export your tasks for integration with other productivity tools or for creating backups.

16. Collaborative Task Lists (Optional): - Share task lists with others for collaborative project management. Assign tasks to team members and track progress together.

By incorporating these steps into your task management routine, you optimize the use of Google Calendar as a centralized hub for scheduling and organizing your activities. The seamless integration of tasks into the calendar view enhances visibility and ensures that your to-do list is closely aligned with your overall schedule.

- **Organizing To-Do Lists**

Organizing your to-do lists efficiently ensures that you can manage tasks with ease and stay on top of your priorities. In Google Calendar, the "Tasks" feature provides a robust platform for creating, organizing, and tracking your to-do lists seamlessly. Here's a comprehensive guide on how to organize your to-do lists effectively:

1. Create Distinct To-Do Lists:

- Utilize the "Tasks" feature to create distinct to-do lists for various aspects of your life, such as work, personal, or specific projects.

2. Assign Due Dates and Times:

- Set due dates and times for each task to prioritize and allocate time for completion.

3. Use Subtasks for Detail:

- Break down complex tasks by adding subtasks. This hierarchical structure provides clarity and helps manage multi-step processes.

4. Categorize Tasks into Lists:

- Assign tasks to specific lists or categories. This can include creating lists for daily tasks, long-term goals, or specific projects.

5. Prioritize Tasks:

- Organize tasks based on priority. Use visual cues such as colors or numbering to indicate the importance or urgency of each task.

6. Drag-and-Drop Reordering:

- Rearrange tasks within a list by using the drag-and-drop feature. Adjust the order to reflect changing priorities.

7. Filter Tasks by List or Due Date:

- Filter tasks in the "Tasks" view based on lists or due dates. This allows you to focus on specific categories or deadlines.

8. View Tasks in Calendar (Optional):

- Toggle the visibility of tasks in the main calendar view to have a holistic view of both events and tasks.

9. Customize Task Colors (Optional):

- Some platforms allow you to customize the colors of tasks. Assign distinct colors to different lists for visual organization.

10. Collaborative Task Lists (Optional): - Share task lists with collaborators for joint project management. Assign tasks to team members and track progress together.

11. Set Reminders for Tasks: - Enhance task management by setting reminders for important tasks. Receive notifications to stay on track.

12. Sync Tasks Across Devices: - Ensure that task synchronization is enabled across your devices. This ensures that your to-do lists are accessible and up-to-date everywhere.

13. Access Tasks on Mobile Devices: - Download the Google Calendar app on your mobile device for convenient access to your tasks on the go.

14. Group Similar Tasks: - Group similar tasks together, either within a list or by assigning the same category or label. This streamlines your focus and makes it easier to tackle related items at once.

15. Daily, Weekly Reviews: - Regularly review and update your to-do lists. Daily or weekly reviews help you reassess priorities and adjust tasks based on changing circumstances.

16. Archive Completed Tasks: - Archive or mark completed tasks as done to maintain a clean and organized to-do list. This declutters your view and provides a sense of accomplishment.

By incorporating these strategies into your to-do list management, you maximize the effectiveness of Google Calendar's "Tasks" feature. This organized approach empowers you to tackle tasks with clarity, stay focused on your goals, and achieve a sense of productivity and accomplishment.

- **Setting Task Priorities and Deadlines**

Effectively setting priorities and deadlines for your tasks is key to successful time management. Google Calendar's "Tasks" feature provides a powerful platform for organizing and managing your to-do lists with precision. Here's a guide on how to strategically set priorities and deadlines for tasks in Google Calendar:

1. Assign Priority Levels:

- Use visual cues such as colors, labels, or numbering to assign priority levels to your tasks. For example, red for high priority, yellow for medium, and green for low.

2. Create Multiple Lists for Priorities:

- Designate separate task lists for different priority levels. This allows you to focus on high-priority tasks without being overwhelmed by less urgent ones.

3. Set Due Dates and Times:

- For each task, set clear due dates and times. This ensures that you allocate specific time slots for task completion.

4. Use Subtasks for Breakdown:

- Break down complex tasks into subtasks and assign due dates to each subtask. This granular approach makes it easier to manage larger projects.

5. Prioritize Based on Importance:

- Prioritize tasks based on their importance and impact on your overall goals. Tackle high-impact tasks first to maximize productivity.

6. Leverage Google Calendar's Color-Coding:

- Utilize Google Calendar's color-coding feature to visually distinguish between tasks with different priorities. This enhances clarity in your task management.

7. Daily, Weekly Priority Assessments:

- Regularly reassess and adjust task priorities. Daily or weekly reviews help you stay adaptable to changing circumstances and shifting priorities.

8. Utilize Reminders for Urgent Tasks:

- Set reminders for urgent or time-sensitive tasks to receive timely notifications. This ensures that you are aware of approaching deadlines.

9. Sync with External Tools (Optional):

- If you use external task management tools, sync them with Google Calendar to maintain consistency and avoid overlooking tasks in different platforms.

10. Group Similar Priority Tasks: - Group tasks with similar priority levels together. This grouping approach allows you to tackle related tasks efficiently.

11. Flexible Scheduling: - Be flexible with task scheduling. Consider time blocks for focused work on high-priority tasks, and allocate buffer time for unexpected interruptions.

12. Set Realistic Deadlines: - Ensure that deadlines are realistic and achievable. Setting unrealistic deadlines can lead to stress and compromise the quality of your work.

13. Use Urgent vs. Important Matrix: - Apply the urgent vs. important matrix to categorize tasks. Focus on tasks that are both urgent and important, but also allocate time for non-urgent but important tasks.

14. Delegate or Postpone Low-Priority Tasks: - Delegate tasks that can be handled by others, and consider postponing low-priority tasks if your schedule is overloaded.

15. Strategic Calendar Views: - Leverage different calendar views in Google Calendar to strategically visualize your tasks. Switch between daily, weekly, and monthly views for a comprehensive perspective.

16. Celebrate Achievements: - Acknowledge and celebrate the completion of high-priority tasks. This positive reinforcement enhances motivation and satisfaction.

By integrating these strategies into your task management approach, you harness the full potential of Google Calendar's "Tasks" feature. Setting priorities and deadlines strategically empowers you to navigate your to-do lists with focus and efficiency, ensuring that you make meaningful progress towards your goals.

- **Syncing Tasks with Other Productivity Apps**

Syncing tasks with other productivity apps enhances your workflow and ensures a seamless experience across different platforms. Google Calendar offers compatibility with various productivity tools, allowing you to centralize and streamline your task management. Here's a guide on how to sync tasks with other productivity apps in Google Calendar:

1. Google Workspace Integration:

- If you use Google Workspace (formerly G Suite), tasks created in Google Calendar seamlessly integrate with other Google Workspace apps, such as Google Docs, Sheets, and Gmail.

2. Google Keep Integration:

- Leverage Google Keep for more detailed notes, checklists, and task management. Tasks created in Google Calendar can be synchronized with Google Keep for additional collaboration features.

3. External Calendar Apps:

- Sync Google Calendar tasks with external calendar apps that support task management features. This ensures that your tasks are accessible across different platforms.

4. Google Tasks Mobile App:

- Download the Google Tasks mobile app to access and manage your tasks on the go. The app provides a dedicated space for comprehensive task management.

5. Third-Party Task Management Apps:

- Explore third-party task management apps that offer integration with Google Calendar. Many apps allow bidirectional syncing, ensuring that updates made in one platform are reflected in the other.

6. Zapier Integrations:

- Use Zapier to create automated workflows (Zaps) that connect Google Calendar tasks with a wide range of productivity apps. This enables customized syncing based on your specific needs.

7. Todoist Integration:

- If you use Todoist for task management, integrate it with Google Calendar to synchronize tasks and deadlines seamlessly. Changes made in either platform are reflected in real-time.

8. Microsoft To-Do Integration:

- If you use Microsoft To-Do, explore integration options to sync tasks with Google Calendar. This ensures that your tasks are visible across both ecosystems.

9. Trello Integration:

- For project management, integrate Trello with Google Calendar to synchronize task cards, deadlines, and project milestones. This enhances collaboration and visibility.

10. Asana Integration: - If you manage tasks in Asana, explore integration settings to sync tasks with Google Calendar. This ensures that your project timelines align with your overall schedule.

11. Evernote Integration: - Integrate Evernote with Google Calendar for seamless syncing of notes, checklists, and task-related details. This provides a consolidated view of your tasks and supporting documentation.

12. Apple Reminders Integration (Optional): - If you use Apple Reminders, explore integration options to sync tasks between Google Calendar and Apple's ecosystem.

13. Calendar Feed: - Generate a calendar feed link for your tasks in Google Calendar. Use this link to integrate tasks with calendar applications that support the iCal format.

14. IFTTT Recipes: - Explore IFTTT (If This Then That) recipes to create custom automations that connect Google Calendar tasks with a wide array of productivity apps and devices.

15. Regularly Review Synced Apps: - Schedule regular reviews to ensure that tasks are syncing correctly across integrated apps. Address any discrepancies or update settings as needed.

16. Test Integration Features: - Test the features and limitations of each integration to ensure that they align with your workflow. Some integrations may have specific functionalities or restrictions.

By incorporating these steps into your task management strategy, you seamlessly integrate Google Calendar tasks with other productivity apps, creating a cohesive and efficient workflow. The flexibility to sync tasks across platforms enhances collaboration, accessibility, and overall productivity.

- **Marking Tasks as Completed**

Celebrating the completion of tasks not only provides a sense of accomplishment but also helps you stay organized and focused on your goals. In Google Calendar, the "Tasks" feature makes it easy to mark tasks as completed. Here's a guide on how to triumphantly mark tasks as done in Google Calendar:

1. Open Google Calendar:

- Ensure you are logged into your Google Account and open Google Calendar.

2. Access "Tasks" View:

- Locate the "Tasks" view in the side panel. If it's not visible, click on the "Tasks" icon to reveal the tasks view.

3. Review Your Tasks:

- In the "Tasks" view, review your list of tasks to identify the ones you've completed.

4. Mark a Task as Completed:

- For each completed task, click the checkbox next to the task to mark it as done. The task will be visually crossed out, indicating completion.

5. Bulk Marking (Optional):

- If you have multiple tasks to mark as completed, use the bulk marking option. Select the tasks you want to mark, and click the "Mark as done" button.

6. Calendar Integration:

- If you have tasks integrated with the main calendar view, completed tasks may be visually distinguished or hidden based on your settings.

7. Mobile Access:

- Download the Google Calendar app on your mobile device to mark tasks as completed on the go.

8. Reflect on Achievements:

- Take a moment to reflect on the tasks you've completed. Acknowledge your achievements and the progress you've made.

9. Archive Completed Tasks:

- Some platforms allow you to archive or move completed tasks to a separate section. This helps keep your task list tidy while preserving a record of accomplishments.

10. Task History (Optional): - Explore task history features if available. Some platforms provide a history log that tracks completed tasks over time.

11. Task Metrics (Optional): - If you're interested in task metrics, consider platforms that provide insights into your task completion trends and productivity patterns.

12. Regular Review: - Schedule regular reviews to ensure that completed tasks are appropriately marked and archived. This contributes to maintaining an organized task list.

13. Synced Apps (Optional): - If you've synced tasks with other productivity apps, check that completed tasks are accurately reflected across all integrated platforms.

14. Celebrate Small Wins: - Celebrate even the smallest victories. Recognizing and celebrating completed tasks boosts motivation and fosters a positive mindset.

15. Task Reassessment: - After marking tasks as completed, reassess your to-do list. Adjust priorities, add new tasks, or refine existing ones based on your evolving goals.

16. Continuous Improvement: - Use the completion of tasks as an opportunity for continuous improvement. Reflect on what worked well and consider adjustments for future tasks.

By embracing the process of marking tasks as completed in Google Calendar, you not only stay organized but also build a record of your accomplishments. This positive reinforcement contributes to a sense of productivity and encourages ongoing success in your task management journey.

CHAPTER 6

TIME BLOCKING TECHNIQUES

- **Understanding Time Blocking**

Time blocking is a powerful productivity technique that involves scheduling dedicated blocks of time for specific tasks or activities. In Google Calendar, mastering time blocking can transform your approach to time management. Here's a comprehensive guide on understanding and implementing time blocking effectively:

1. Open Google Calendar:

- Ensure you are logged into your Google Account and open Google Calendar.

2. Choose a Calendar View:

- Select the calendar view that suits your planning style. Choose between daily, weekly, or monthly views to visualize your schedule.

3. Identify Key Priorities:

- Identify the key tasks or activities that require focused attention. These can include work projects, personal goals, or recurring commitments.

4. Create Dedicated Time Blocks:

- Allocate dedicated time blocks for each identified priority. Click and drag to create blocks on the calendar for specific tasks.

5. Use Different Colors (Optional):

- Enhance visual clarity by using different colors for various types of tasks or categories. This color-coding technique allows for easy identification.

6. Prioritize High-Impact Tasks:

- Place high-impact or priority tasks in prime time slots when you are most alert and focused. Reserve these times for your most important work.

7. Include Breaks and Buffer Time:

- Integrate breaks and buffer time between tasks to avoid burnout and accommodate unexpected delays. This ensures a realistic and sustainable schedule.

8. Time Blocking for Meetings:

- Allocate specific time blocks for meetings. This prevents meetings from interrupting your workflow and allows for efficient coordination.

9. Batch Similar Tasks:

- Group similar tasks together within a time block. Batching tasks of a similar nature minimizes context-switching and enhances efficiency.

10. Be Realistic with Time Estimates: - Be realistic when estimating the time needed for each task. Avoid overloading your schedule to ensure a manageable workload.

11. Adjustable Time Blocks: - Embrace flexibility by making time blocks adjustable. Drag and resize blocks to accommodate changes in priorities or unexpected events.

12. Integrate Personal Activities: - Include personal activities, self-care, or hobbies in your time blocks. Balancing work and personal life contributes to overall well-being.

13. Daily Planning Routine: - Establish a daily planning routine to review and adjust time blocks as needed. This proactive approach enhances adaptability and responsiveness.

14. Include Downtime (Optional): - Allocate downtime or reflection time within your schedule. This provides moments for relaxation and mental recharge.

15. Reflect on Time Block Effectiveness: - Regularly reflect on the effectiveness of your time blocks. Adjust your approach based on what works best for your productivity and focus.

16. Sync with Other Apps (Optional): - If you use external productivity apps, ensure that your time blocks are synced across platforms. This allows for a cohesive and synchronized approach.

By mastering time blocking in Google Calendar, you gain control over your schedule, enhance focus, and optimize productivity. The intentional allocation of time to specific tasks ensures that you make meaningful progress toward your goals while maintaining a balanced and sustainable work-life rhythm.

- **Implementing Time Blocking in Google Calendar**

Time blocking is a transformative technique that maximizes your productivity by allocating dedicated blocks of time to specific tasks or activities. In Google Calendar, implementing time blocking is straightforward and empowers you to take control of your schedule. Here's a step-by-step guide on how to effectively implement time blocking in Google Calendar:

1. Open Google Calendar:

- Ensure you are logged into your Google Account and open Google Calendar.

2. Choose a Calendar View:

- Select the calendar view that aligns with your planning preferences. Options include daily, weekly, or monthly views.

3. Identify Priorities:

- Identify your key priorities for the day or week. These can be work projects, personal goals, or recurring commitments.

4. Create Time Blocks:

- Click and drag on the desired time slots to create dedicated time blocks for each priority. The length of the block should align with the time you estimate for the task.

5. Utilize Different Colors (Optional):

- Enhance visual organization by using different colors for various tasks or categories. Right-click on a time block, select "Event color," and choose the color that corresponds to the task.

6. Prioritize High-Impact Tasks:

- Place high-impact or priority tasks during your most productive hours. Reserve prime time slots for work that requires intense focus and creativity.

7. Include Breaks and Buffer Time:

- Integrate breaks and buffer time between tasks to prevent burnout and accommodate unforeseen delays. This ensures a realistic and sustainable schedule.

8. Time Blocking for Meetings:

- Allocate specific time blocks for meetings, preventing them from disrupting your workflow. Clearly define when you are available for meetings.

9. Batch Similar Tasks:

- Group similar tasks together within a time block. Batching similar tasks minimizes context-switching and boosts efficiency.

10. Be Realistic with Time Estimates: - Provide realistic time estimates for each task to avoid overloading your schedule. Consider factors like task complexity and potential interruptions.

11. Adjustable Time Blocks: - Embrace flexibility by making time blocks adjustable. Drag and resize blocks to accommodate changes in priorities or unexpected events.

12. Integrate Personal Activities: - Include personal activities, self-care, or hobbies in your time blocks. Balancing work and personal life contributes to overall well-being.

13. Daily Planning Routine: - Establish a daily planning routine to review and adjust time blocks. This proactive approach enhances adaptability and responsiveness.

14. Include Downtime (Optional): - Allocate downtime or reflection time within your schedule. These moments provide relaxation and mental recharge.

15. Reflect on Time Block Effectiveness: - Regularly reflect on the effectiveness of your time blocks. Adjust your approach based on what works best for your productivity and focus.

16. Sync with Other Apps (Optional): - If you use external productivity apps, ensure that your time blocks are synced across platforms. This allows for a cohesive and synchronized approach.

By following these steps, you seamlessly integrate time blocking into your Google Calendar, transforming the way you manage your time. The intentional allocation of time to specific tasks ensures that you make meaningful progress toward your goals while maintaining a balanced and sustainable work-life rhythm.

- **Balancing Work and Personal Life**

Balancing work and personal life is essential for overall well-being and sustained productivity. Google Calendar serves as a powerful ally in achieving this balance by providing tools to organize, prioritize, and protect your time. Here's a guide on how to harmonize your work and personal life using Google Calendar:

1. Create Separate Calendars:

- Utilize multiple calendars within Google Calendar to distinguish between work and personal commitments. Assign different colors to each for visual clarity.

2. Set Boundaries with Work Hours:

- Establish clear work hours and mark them on your calendar. This helps set boundaries and communicates your availability to colleagues and friends.

3. Block Personal Time:

- Reserve dedicated time blocks for personal activities, hobbies, or self-care. Treat these as non-negotiable commitments to ensure a balanced lifestyle.

4. Prioritize Self-Care:

- Allocate specific time for self-care routines, exercise, and relaxation. Treat these as important appointments, just like work meetings.

5. Leverage "Out of Office" Feature:

- When taking personal time or vacations, use the "Out of Office" feature to inform colleagues and prevent work-related interruptions.

6. Separate Work and Personal To-Do Lists:

- If using Google Calendar's "Tasks" feature, maintain separate task lists for work and personal tasks. This helps maintain focus and clarity.

7. Color-Coded Events and Tasks:

- Color-code work and personal events or tasks to quickly differentiate between the two. This visual cue enhances organization and balance.

8. Sync with Personal Apps:

- Integrate Google Calendar with personal apps and platforms to ensure that personal commitments are seamlessly reflected in your schedule.

9. Family Calendar for Shared Events:

- Create a family calendar to coordinate and share events with family members. This promotes transparency and helps in planning shared activities.

10. Time Blocking for Personal Goals: - Use time blocking to dedicate specific time to personal goals, whether they are related to hobbies, learning, or other non-work aspirations.

11. Set Realistic Workload: - Avoid overloading your work schedule. Set realistic expectations for your workload to prevent burnout and allow time for personal pursuits.

12. Use Notifications Wisely: - Customize notifications to align with your preferences. Ensure that work-related notifications don't intrude into personal time and vice versa.

13. Flexible Scheduling: - Embrace flexible scheduling to accommodate personal and family needs. Adjust work hours or deadlines when necessary to maintain balance.

14. Regular Review and Reflection: - Schedule regular reviews to assess your work-life balance. Reflect on adjustments needed to ensure that both aspects of your life are thriving.

15. Share Calendars with Family: - Share your personal calendar with family members to enhance coordination. This ensures everyone is aware of each other's commitments.

16. Learn to Say No: - Develop the ability to say no to additional work commitments when your schedule is full. Prioritize your well-being and personal time.

By implementing these strategies, you leverage the organizational prowess of Google Calendar to harmonize your work and personal life. Striking a balance ensures that you thrive both professionally and personally, fostering a fulfilling and sustainable lifestyle.

- **Maximizing Focus and Productivity**

In a world filled with distractions, honing your focus is a superpower. Google Calendar becomes your ally in this quest, helping you structure your time for peak productivity. Here's a guide on how to maximize your focus and productivity using Google Calendar:

1. Time Blocking for Deep Work:

- Dedicate specific time blocks for deep, focused work. During these intervals, eliminate distractions and immerse yourself in high-priority tasks.

2. Set Clear Priorities:

- Use Google Calendar to prioritize tasks. Assign different colors to tasks based on their urgency or importance, creating a visual hierarchy.

3. Calendar Notifications:

- Customize calendar notifications to alert you before important tasks or meetings. This proactive approach helps you prepare and transition smoothly.

4. Limit Meeting Times:

- Set specific time slots for meetings to prevent them from dominating your entire day. This leaves ample time for focused, uninterrupted work.

5. Integrate with Task Management:

- Integrate Google Calendar with task management tools. This synergy ensures that your to-do list aligns seamlessly with your scheduled time blocks.

6. Leverage "Do Not Disturb" Mode:

- Activate "Do Not Disturb" mode during critical work periods. This silences notifications, creating an environment conducive to concentration.

7. Block Out Focus Periods:

- Clearly mark focus periods on your calendar. This signals to colleagues that you are unavailable during these times, fostering respect for your focused work.

8. Break Down Tasks with Sub-Categories:

- Use sub-categories or labels within Google Calendar to break down complex tasks. This enhances clarity and allows you to tackle tasks in manageable increments.

9. Regular Reviews and Adjustments:

- Schedule regular reviews of your calendar to assess your focus and productivity levels. Adjust your strategy based on what works best for you.

10. Pomodoro Technique: - Implement the Pomodoro Technique by scheduling focused work sessions followed by short breaks. Google Calendar's timed events align perfectly with this method.

11. Declutter Your Calendar: - Keep your calendar clutter-free. Remove unnecessary or low-priority events to create a clean visual space that supports focused work.

12. Use Week and Month Views Strategically: - Switch between week and month views to strategically plan your focus periods. Week views offer detailed planning, while month views provide a broader perspective.

13. Mindful Transition Times: - Allocate transition times between tasks to decompress and prepare for the next activity. This mindful approach maintains a steady pace throughout your day.

14. Batch Similar Tasks: - Group similar tasks together in designated time blocks. Batching tasks minimizes cognitive load and enhances efficiency.

15. Set Realistic Expectations: - Avoid overcommitting. Set realistic expectations for your daily schedule to ensure that you can fully focus on each task without rushing.

16. Reflect and Celebrate Wins: - Regularly reflect on your accomplishments. Celebrate small wins to reinforce positive habits and maintain motivation.

By incorporating these strategies into your routine, you leverage the full potential of Google Calendar to enhance focus and productivity. The intentional structuring of your time allows you to navigate the demands of your day with purpose and efficiency.

- **Adjusting and Fine-Tuning Your Time Blocks**

Flexibility is a key element in effective time management. Google Calendar empowers you to refine your schedule with ease. Here's a guide on adjusting and fine-tuning your time blocks to align with your evolving priorities:

1. Open Google Calendar:

- Log in to your Google Account and open Google Calendar.

2. Choose a Calendar View:

- Select the calendar view that suits your planning needs. Daily, weekly, and monthly views offer different perspectives on your schedule.

3. Review Your Current Schedule:

- Assess your existing time blocks and events. Identify areas that may need adjustment based on changing priorities.

4. Drag and Drop to Reschedule:

- To adjust a time block, simply click and drag it to a new time slot. This intuitive feature allows for quick rescheduling.

5. Resize Time Blocks:

- Fine-tune the duration of a time block by clicking and dragging its edges. This flexibility ensures that your schedule aligns with the actual time needed for tasks.

6. Use the "Edit Event" Option:

- Right-click on a time block and select "Edit event" to access detailed options. Here, you can modify the title, time, color, and other specifics.

7. Adjust Notifications:

- If you need to change notification settings for a specific time block, access the event details and customize the notification preferences.

8. Delete or Duplicate Blocks:

- Remove a time block by clicking on it and selecting "Delete." Alternatively, duplicate blocks for recurring tasks by copying and pasting or using the "Duplicate" option.

9. Integrate Breaks:

- Fine-tune your breaks by adjusting their duration and placement. Ensure that breaks align with your natural energy levels and provide necessary rest.

10. Prioritize High-Impact Tasks: - If new high-impact tasks arise, prioritize them by adjusting your schedule. Ensure that your most crucial work aligns with your peak focus times.

11. Utilize Keyboard Shortcuts: - Speed up the fine-tuning process by using keyboard shortcuts. Familiarize yourself with shortcuts for navigation, editing, and adjusting time blocks.

12. Color Code for Clarity: - Enhance visual clarity by using different colors for various types of tasks or categories. This makes it easy to identify and prioritize at a glance.

13. Sync with Task Management Tools: - If you use external task management tools, ensure that adjustments in Google Calendar sync seamlessly with your task lists.

14. Collaborate with Colleagues: - For collaborative projects, coordinate with colleagues by adjusting shared time blocks. This ensures that everyone is aligned with the latest schedule.

15. Regularly Review and Update: - Schedule regular reviews to assess the effectiveness of your time blocks. Make adjustments based on your evolving priorities and workload.

16. Reflect on Productivity Patterns: - Reflect on your productivity patterns and energy levels. Fine-tune your schedule to accommodate tasks that align with your natural rhythms.

By embracing the adaptability of Google Calendar, you optimize your time management strategy. The ability to adjust and fine-tune your time blocks ensures that your schedule remains dynamic, responsive, and aligned with your goals.

CHAPTER 7

TROUBLESHOOTING AND TIPS

- **Common Issues and Solutions**

Even the most reliable tools can face occasional hiccups. Google Calendar syncing issues can disrupt your workflow, but fret not—here are common problems and their solutions to keep your schedule running smoothly:

1. Syncing Delays:

- **Issue:** Changes made in Google Calendar take time to reflect across devices.

- **Solution:** Check your internet connection. If the issue persists, manually refresh the calendar or sign out and sign back in.

2. Events Not Syncing:

- **Issue:** Newly created events or updates are not appearing on other synced devices.

- **Solution:** Ensure that all devices are connected to the internet. Manually sync calendars on each device, and check for any conflicting events.

3. Duplicate Events:

- **Issue:** Events are duplicated across devices, leading to confusion.
- **Solution:** Review third-party app integrations. Disable unnecessary plugins or apps that might be causing duplication. Manually remove duplicates.

4. Missing Events:

- **Issue:** Some events are not showing up on certain devices.
- **Solution:** Confirm that the calendar containing the events is selected and visible on all devices. Check for calendar filters that might be hiding specific events.

5. Incorrect Time Zones:

- **Issue:** Events appear at different times on different devices.
- **Solution:** Verify that all devices are set to the correct time zone. Adjust the time zone settings in Google Calendar and on your devices if needed.

6. Syncing with External Calendars:

- **Issue:** Trouble syncing Google Calendar with external calendars.

- **Solution:** Double-check the external calendar settings. Ensure that the sharing settings are configured correctly, and refresh the calendar subscription if necessary.

7. Mobile App Syncing Issues:

- **Issue:** Google Calendar on mobile is not syncing properly.
- **Solution:** Update the app to the latest version. Check the sync settings within the app and ensure that the correct calendars are selected for synchronization.

8. Syncing with Task Management Apps:

- **Issue:** Google Calendar tasks are not syncing with external task management apps.
- **Solution:** Review the integration settings for task management apps. Reauthorize the connection if needed and ensure that the correct task lists are selected.

9. Shared Calendar Syncing:

- **Issue:** Shared calendars are not syncing with collaborators.
- **Solution:** Verify that sharing settings are configured correctly. Collaborators should have the appropriate permissions to view and edit the calendar.

10. Network Connection Issues: - **Issue:** Syncing problems persist despite troubleshooting. - **Solution:** Check your network connection. If using a mobile device, switch between Wi-Fi and cellular data. Restart your router if necessary.

11. Google Account Sync Issues: - **Issue:** General syncing issues with multiple Google services. - **Solution:** Confirm that your Google Account settings are up to date. Reauthorize the account on the affected devices and check for any service outages.

12. Calendar App Updates: - **Issue:** Syncing problems after a calendar app update. - **Solution:** Ensure that all devices are using the latest version of the calendar app. Updates often include bug fixes that address syncing issues.

13. Calendar Notifications Not Syncing: - **Issue:** Calendar notifications are not consistent across devices. - **Solution:** Check notification settings on each device. Ensure that notifications are enabled for events and that the settings are consistent.

14. Data Security: - **Issue:** Concerns about the security of synced data. - **Solution:** Regularly review and update your security settings. Use two-factor authentication for added protection and be cautious when granting third-party app access.

15. Consult Google Support: - **Issue:** Persistent syncing problems with no apparent solution. - **Solution:** Reach out to Google Support for assistance. They can provide personalized guidance based on your specific situation.

By addressing these common syncing issues and applying the suggested solutions, you can maintain a seamless and reliable syncing experience with Google Calendar across all your devices.

- **Managing Notifications Effectively**

Notifications are your trusty allies in staying on top of your schedule. Google Calendar offers versatile notification settings to ensure you never miss a beat. Here's a guide on managing notifications effectively:

1. Customizing Event Notifications:

- **How to:** Open an event, click "Edit," and navigate to the "Notifications" section. Customize notifications based on your preferences—choose email, pop-up, or mobile notifications.

2. Multiple Reminders for Important Events:

- **How to:** Set multiple reminders for crucial events. Combine pop-up reminders with email notifications to reinforce the importance of upcoming tasks.

3. Adjusting Default Notification Settings:

- **How to:** Access Google Calendar settings, go to "Event settings," and customize default notification preferences. This streamlines the process for new events.

4. Snooze and Dismiss Options:

- **How to:** When a notification pops up, utilize the snooze option for a gentle reminder later. Dismiss notifications for events that no longer require your immediate attention.

5. Mobile App Push Notifications:

- **How to:** Enable push notifications on the mobile app for real-time updates on your device. This ensures you receive timely reminders even when the app is closed.

6. Email Digests for Daily Agendas:

- **How to:** Set up daily email digests summarizing your agenda. This consolidated email provides a comprehensive overview of the day's events.

7. Declutter with Time-Bound Notifications:

- **How to:** Limit pop-up notifications to a specific time window before an event. This prevents early notifications and minimizes distractions.

8. Email Notifications for Calendar Changes:

- **How to:** Receive email notifications for changes made to shared calendars. Stay informed about updates made by collaborators.

9. Disabling Notifications for Specific Calendars:

- **How to:** Turn off notifications for less critical calendars. This declutters your notification feed and ensures you focus on high-priority events.

10. Browser Notifications for Web Users: - How to: Enable browser notifications for Google Calendar on your desktop. Stay informed even when the calendar tab is not actively open.

11. Setting Default Notification Times: - How to: Customize default notification times for various events. This ensures consistency in your notification preferences.

12. Attendee Notifications for Events: - How to: When creating events with attendees, set up notifications for them. This fosters better coordination and ensures everyone is on the same page.

13. Location-Based Notifications: - How to: Enable location-based notifications for events. Receive a reminder when you arrive or leave a specified location, enhancing event awareness.

14. Syncing Notifications Across Devices: - How to: Ensure that notification settings are synced across all your devices. This consistency prevents discrepancies in receiving timely alerts.

15. Review and Adjust Regularly: - How to: Schedule periodic reviews of your notification settings. Adjust them based on changes in your routine and evolving preferences.

16. Use "Find a Time" Feature for Efficient Scheduling: - How to: Leverage the "Find a Time" feature when creating events with multiple participants. This helps find mutually available time slots, streamlining scheduling.

By mastering these notification hacks, you elevate your awareness of events and deadlines, ensuring a well-managed and organized schedule with Google Calendar.

Google Calendar Hacks for Power Users: Unleashing Advanced Features

Become a Google Calendar power user with these hacks that unveil advanced features and functionalities, elevating your scheduling game:

1. Time Zone Management:

- **Hack:** Easily manage events across different time zones. Set specific time zones for events to avoid confusion, especially when collaborating with individuals in other regions.

2. Keyboard Shortcuts:

- **Hack:** Speed up navigation and event creation with keyboard shortcuts. Familiarize yourself with commands like "c" to create a new event and "t" to switch to today's date.

3. Quick Event Creation:

- **Hack:** Create events swiftly using natural language. Type phrases like "Meeting with John tomorrow at 2 pm" directly into the "Create" box for instant event generation.

4. Agenda Integration:

- **Hack:** Integrate your Google Calendar with Google Workspace tools like Gmail and Google Meet. Access your agenda seamlessly within these applications for efficient planning.

5. Add Attachments to Events:

- **Hack:** Attach relevant files to events directly from Google Drive. This centralizes event-related documents for easy access.

6. Embed Google Calendar on Websites:

- **Hack:** Share your calendar publicly or embed it on websites. This is particularly useful for displaying public events or schedules.

7. Discover Interesting Calendars:

- **Hack:** Explore and subscribe to interesting calendars from the "Browse Calendars of Interest" section. Stay informed about holidays, sports events, and more.

8. Time Block with "Working Hours":

- **Hack:** Utilize the "Working Hours" feature to set specific time blocks for focused work. This ensures that events are automatically scheduled during your designated working hours.

9. Color Coding Beyond Basics:

- **Hack:** Take color coding to the next level by assigning colors based on project categories or priority levels. This visual strategy enhances organizational clarity.

10. Import and Export Calendars: - Hack: Import external calendars or export your Google Calendar for backup or sharing purposes. This feature facilitates seamless integration with other platforms.

11. SMS Reminders: - Hack: Receive event reminders via SMS. Enable this option in the notification settings for timely alerts on your mobile device.

12. Hide Declined Events: - Hack: Declined an invitation? Hide declined events to declutter your calendar view. This keeps the focus on confirmed commitments.

13. Create Appointment Slots: - Hack: Use the "Appointment Slots" feature to open specific time blocks for appointments. This is ideal for scheduling one-on-one meetings or office hours.

14. View Multiple Time Zones: - Hack: Enable the "World Clock" feature to view multiple time zones simultaneously. This is invaluable for coordinating with individuals in different regions.

15. Email Guests Directly: - Hack: Email event guests directly from Google Calendar. This feature streamlines communication and ensures everyone is on the same page.

16. Explore Labs Features: - Hack: Check out experimental features in Google Calendar Labs. While not officially supported, these features can offer additional functionalities for those who enjoy testing new tools.

With these advanced hacks, you'll navigate Google Calendar with finesse, unlocking features that cater to your unique scheduling needs.

Staying Ahead: Keeping Updated on New Google Calendar Features and Updates

Google Calendar evolves continuously, introducing new features and enhancements. Stay ahead of the curve by staying informed about the latest updates:

1. Official Google Blog:

- **Stay Updated:** Regularly visit the Official Google Blog for announcements about Google Calendar updates and new features.

2. Google Workspace Updates:

- **Stay Updated:** Subscribe to the Google Workspace Updates Blog for detailed information on updates across the Google Workspace, including Calendar.

3. Release Notes in Google Calendar Help:

- **Stay Updated:** Explore the Release Notes section in Google Calendar Help. This provides a detailed history of updates and changes.

4. Follow Google Workspace on Social Media:

- **Stay Updated:** Follow Google Workspace on social media platforms such as Twitter and LinkedIn for real-time updates.

5. Google Calendar Help Center:

- **Stay Updated:** Regularly check the Google Calendar Help Center for articles, guides, and announcements related to new features.

6. Google Calendar Community Forum:

- **Stay Updated:** Join the Google Calendar Community Forum to engage with other users, discuss updates, and get insights into the latest features.

7. Beta Testing Programs:

- **Stay Updated:** Consider participating in Google Calendar beta testing programs if available. Beta users often get early access to new features and can provide valuable feedback.

8. Webinars and Training Sessions:

- **Stay Updated:** Attend webinars or training sessions organized by Google Workspace. These sessions often cover new features and best practices for using Google Calendar effectively.

9. Email Notifications from Google Workspace:

- **Stay Updated:** Ensure that you receive email notifications from Google Workspace regarding updates and new features. Check your email preferences to stay informed.

10. Google Calendar App Updates: - Stay Updated: Regularly update the Google Calendar app on your mobile devices. App updates often include new features and improvements.

11. Podcasts and Blogs on Productivity: - Stay Updated: Explore productivity-focused podcasts and blogs. These platforms often discuss and review the latest tools and features, including those in Google Calendar.

12. Google Workspace YouTube Channel: - Stay Updated: Subscribe to the Google Workspace YouTube Channel for video updates and tutorials on new features in Google Calendar.

13. Community Feedback and Forums: - Stay Updated: Engage with the Google Calendar user community. Forums and community feedback often highlight user experiences with new features.

14. Google Workspace Status Dashboard: - Stay Updated: Check the Google Workspace Status Dashboard for information on service disruptions, updates, and resolutions.

15. Set Google Calendar Preferences for Updates: - Stay Updated: Adjust your Google Calendar settings to receive notifications about new features and updates directly within the app.

By actively seeking information through these channels, you ensure that you're always aware of the latest enhancements to

Google Calendar, maximizing your efficiency and optimizing your scheduling experience.

CHAPTER 8

ADVANCED FEATURES AND FUTURE TRENDS

- **Exploring Labs Features**

Google Calendar Labs serves as a playground for experimental features that can enhance your calendar experience. Delve into these Labs features to discover hidden gems and optimize your scheduling prowess:

1. Accessing Google Calendar Labs:

- **Exploration:** Navigate to Google Calendar settings, find the "Labs" tab, and explore the available experimental features.

2. Background Image:

- **Feature:** Personalize your calendar by adding a custom background image.
- **How to Enable:** In Labs, activate the "Background image" feature and upload your preferred image.

3. Gentle Reminders:

- **Feature:** Receive reminders without disruptive pop-ups or sounds.

- **How to Enable:** Turn on "Gentle reminders" in Labs for a subtler notification experience.

4. Jump to Date:

- **Feature:** Quickly navigate to a specific date in your calendar.
- **How to Enable:** Activate "Jump to date" in Labs, allowing for efficient date selection.

5. Hide Morning and Night:

- **Feature:** Streamline your daily view by hiding morning and night hours.
- **How to Enable:** Use "Hide morning and night" to focus on your active hours.

6. World Clock:

- **Feature:** View multiple time zones simultaneously within Google Calendar.
- **How to Enable:** Turn on "World Clock" in Labs to display additional time zone information.

7. Next Meeting:

- **Feature:** Quickly view information about your upcoming meeting directly on the calendar.

- **How to Enable:** Activate "Next meeting" in Labs for at-a-glance meeting details.

8. Free or Busy Information:

- **Feature:** See whether attendees are available or busy during event scheduling.
- **How to Enable:** Enable "Free or busy information" in Labs for enhanced scheduling insights.

9. Hide Weekends:

- **Feature:** Declutter your calendar view by hiding weekends.
- **How to Enable:** Use "Hide weekends" in Labs for a focused workweek view.

10. Extra Calendars: - **Feature:** Display additional calendars beyond the default ones. - **How to Enable:** Activate "Extra calendars" in Labs to include more calendars in your view.

11. Multiple Calendars in Day View: - **Feature:** Show events from multiple calendars in the day view. - **How to Enable:** Enable "Multiple calendars in day view" for a comprehensive daily overview.

12. Year View: - **Feature:** Gain a broader perspective with a year view of your calendar. - **How to Enable:** Turn on "Year view" in Labs for an annual snapshot.

13. Event Flair: - **Feature:** Add icons or "flair" to events for visual distinction. - **How to Enable:** Activate "Event flair" in Labs to enhance event categorization.

14. Hide Invitations: - **Feature:** Declutter your calendar by hiding event invitations. - **How to Enable:** Use "Hide invitations" in Labs to focus on confirmed events.

15. Event Attachments: - **Feature:** Attach files directly to calendar events. - **How to Enable:** Turn on "Event attachments" in Labs to include attachments with event details.

16. Weather Calendar: - **Feature:** Integrate weather information into your calendar events. - **How to Enable:** Enable "Weather Calendar" in Labs for weather updates within your calendar.

Explore these Labs features to tailor your Google Calendar experience, uncovering functionalities that align with your unique scheduling preferences.

Tailoring Your Experience: Customization with Google Calendar Extensions and Add-ons

Extend the functionality of Google Calendar by incorporating extensions and add-ons that cater to your specific needs. Customize your calendar experience with these versatile tools:

1. Google Calendar Extensions:

- **Customization:** Explore browser extensions that enhance Google Calendar features.
- **Examples:** "Checker Plus for Google Calendar" (Chrome) or "Simple Calendar" (Firefox).

2. Zapier Integration:

- **Customization:** Connect Google Calendar with other apps using Zapier.
- **Examples:** Automate tasks by creating Zaps that trigger actions based on calendar events.

3. Calendar Templates:

- **Customization:** Use calendar templates for specific purposes.
- **Examples:** Explore templates for project management, fitness routines, or meal planning.

4. Google Workspace Marketplace:

- **Customization:** Browse the Google Workspace Marketplace for a variety of calendar-related extensions and add-ons.

5. Appointment Scheduling Tools:

- **Customization:** Integrate appointment scheduling tools directly into Google Calendar.
- **Examples:** Tools like Calendly or Doodle streamline the process of setting up meetings.

6. Google Calendar Add-ons:

- **Customization:** Enhance Google Calendar with add-ons that offer additional features.
- **Examples:** Explore add-ons like "Checker Plus for Google Calendar" or "Gmelius" for collaborative features.

7. Email Integration:

- **Customization:** Integrate your email and calendar for seamless communication.
- **Examples:** Tools like "Boomerang" allow you to schedule emails and sync them with your calendar.

8. Task Management Integration:

- **Customization:** Connect your task management tools with Google Calendar.
- **Examples:** Apps like Todoist or Microsoft To Do integrate seamlessly for unified task tracking.

9. Google Meet Enhancements:

- **Customization:** Improve your Google Meet experience directly from Google Calendar.
- **Examples:** Extensions like "Google Meet Grid View" provide additional functionality during video meetings.

10. Mobile Apps for On-the-Go Access: - Customization: Install mobile apps that complement Google Calendar. - **Examples:** Apps like "Business Calendar 2" (Android) or "Fantastical" (iOS) offer advanced features.

11. Calendar Analytics Tools: - Customization: Gain insights into your time management with analytics tools. - **Examples:** Tools like "Clockwise" provide analytics on your calendar patterns and suggest optimal scheduling.

12. Chrome Browser Extensions: - Customization: Enhance your Google Calendar experience with Chrome extensions. - **Examples:** "Checker Plus for Google Calendar" or "Google Calendar (by Google)" provide additional features and ease of access.

13. Mobile Calendar Widgets: - Customization: Customize your mobile device's home screen with calendar widgets. - **Examples:** Widgets like "Month: Calendar Widget" (Android) or "Fantastical" (iOS) provide at-a-glance information.

14. Focus and Productivity Tools: - **Customization:** Use tools that integrate with Google Calendar to boost focus. - **Examples:** Apps like "Forest" or "StayFocusd" can complement your calendar for enhanced productivity.

15. Time Tracking Integrations: - **Customization:** Track and analyze your time usage directly from Google Calendar. - **Examples:** Apps like "Toggl" integrate seamlessly for time tracking purposes.

16. AI-Powered Calendar Assistants: - **Customization:** Explore AI-driven assistants that enhance your scheduling. - **Examples:** "x.ai" uses artificial intelligence to schedule meetings on your behalf.

By incorporating these extensions and add-ons, you tailor your Google Calendar experience to suit your unique workflow and preferences, unlocking a more personalized and efficient scheduling tool.

- **Voice Commands and Smart Assistant Integration**

Effortlessly manage your schedule by harnessing the power of voice commands and seamless integration with smart assistants. Here's how you can optimize your Google Calendar experience:

1. Voice Commands on Mobile Devices:

- **Integration:** Activate voice commands on your mobile device (e.g., "Hey Google" on Android or "Hey Siri" on iOS) to create, edit, or check events on the go.

2. Smart Assistant Integration:

- **Integration:** Connect Google Calendar with smart assistants like Google Assistant, Amazon Alexa, or Apple's Siri. Use natural language commands to interact with your calendar.

3. Creating Events with Voice:

- **How to:** Simply say, "Add an event to my calendar" followed by event details like date, time, and location. The smart assistant translates your spoken words into actionable calendar events.

4. Checking Your Agenda:

- **How to:** Ask your smart assistant, "What's on my agenda today?" or "What's next on my calendar?" to receive spoken summaries of your upcoming events.

5. Setting Reminders:

- **How to:** Use voice commands to set reminders for important tasks or events. For example, say, "Remind me to prepare for the meeting tomorrow at 3 PM."

6. Sending Invitations:

- **How to:** Dictate invitations for meetings or events by specifying details like date, time, and participants. The smart assistant takes care of sending invites on your behalf.

7. Voice-Activated Time Blocking:

- **How to:** Experiment with voice-activated time blocking. Command your smart assistant to block specific time slots for focused work or breaks.

8. Hands-Free Meeting Joining:

- **How to:** Seamlessly join virtual meetings by instructing your smart assistant to "Join the next meeting on my calendar." The assistant can handle the connection details.

9. Natural Language Processing:

- **Integration:** Leverage natural language processing capabilities of smart assistants. Speak conversationally when interacting with your calendar, and the assistant interprets your intentions accurately.

10. Daily Briefings: - How to: Receive daily briefings from your smart assistant summarizing the day's events, tasks, and important deadlines.

11. Location-Based Commands: - How to: Incorporate location-based commands. For example, instruct your smart assistant to "Remind me of my shopping list when I'm near the grocery store."

12. Multilingual Support: - Integration: Explore multilingual support in smart assistants. Interact with your calendar using voice commands in different languages.

13. Calendar Insights through Conversations: - Integration: Engage in conversations with your smart assistant to gain insights into your calendar patterns, preferences, and suggested improvements.

14. Hands-Free Rescheduling: - How to: Reschedule events with ease by saying, "Move my meeting to tomorrow at 2 PM" or similar voice commands.

15. Voice-Enabled Collaboration: - Integration: Collaborate with others by instructing your smart assistant to schedule meetings, check availability, or send calendar invites on behalf of a team.

16. Continuous Learning and Adaptation: - Integration: Embrace smart assistants that continuously learn from your interactions. Over time, the assistant becomes more adept at understanding your preferences and managing your calendar efficiently.

By seamlessly integrating voice commands and smart assistants into your Google Calendar routine, you streamline the scheduling process and enhance the overall efficiency of your time management.

Machine Learning Unleashed: Transforming Time Management with Google Calendar

Machine learning revolutionizes time management by bringing intelligent automation and personalized insights to Google Calendar. Explore the transformative impact of machine learning in optimizing your schedule:

1. Smart Scheduling Assistance:

- **Integration:** Benefit from smart scheduling assistance powered by machine learning. Google Calendar suggests optimal meeting times based on participants' availability and preferences.

2. Predictive Event Creation:

- **How it Works:** Machine learning algorithms analyze your past scheduling behaviors to predict and propose new events. The system learns your preferences over time, streamlining event creation.

3. Personalized Time Blocking:

- **Integration:** Experience personalized time blocking recommendations. Machine learning considers your work patterns, productivity peaks, and preferences to suggest effective time blocks.

4. Contextual Calendar Insights:

- **How it Works:** Machine learning algorithms provide contextual insights into your calendar. Understand the impact of events on your productivity and make informed decisions.

5. Adaptive Notifications:

- **Integration:** Leverage adaptive notifications that learn from your responsiveness and prioritize alerts accordingly. Machine learning ensures that important reminders receive the attention they deserve.

6. Automated Meeting Preparations:

- **How it Works:** Machine learning automates meeting preparations by analyzing event details, suggesting relevant documents, and providing insights into the meeting agenda.

7. Dynamic Event Duration Suggestions:

- **Integration:** Experience dynamic event duration suggestions. Machine learning considers the nature of events and past behavior to propose suitable time allocations.

8. Intelligent Rescheduling Assistance:

- **How it Works:** Machine learning assists in intelligent event rescheduling. The system takes into account your priorities, conflicts, and preferences to propose alternative times.

9. Sentiment Analysis for Productivity:

- **Integration:** Employ sentiment analysis to gauge the emotional impact of events on your productivity. Machine learning identifies patterns and suggests adjustments for a balanced schedule.

10. Learning from Calendar Interactions: - How it Works: Machine learning algorithms learn from your calendar interactions, adapting to changes in your routine, preferences, and priorities.

11. Natural Language Understanding: - Integration: Embrace natural language understanding in event creation. Machine learning enables Google Calendar to comprehend and interpret natural language commands for effortless scheduling.

12. Collaborative Scheduling Optimization: - How it Works: Machine learning optimizes collaborative scheduling. The system learns from the preferences and availability of multiple participants to suggest meeting times that accommodate everyone.

13. Event Category Suggestions: - Integration: Machine learning categorizes events based on patterns and context. This simplifies the organization of your calendar and provides insights into the distribution of your time.

14. Time Management Analytics: - How it Works: Machine learning-driven analytics offer deep insights into your time management habits. Identify trends, evaluate productivity levels, and receive suggestions for improvement.

15. Adaptive Work-Break Balancing: - Integration: Machine learning balances work and break intervals. The system suggests optimal durations for focused work sessions and recommends appropriate break times.

16. Continuous Learning and Adaptation: - Integration: Experience continuous learning and adaptation. Machine learning models evolve with each interaction, ensuring that your Google Calendar becomes increasingly tailored to your unique needs.

As machine learning continues to advance, the integration of intelligent algorithms into Google Calendar promises a future where time management becomes not just efficient but deeply personalized.

The Future of Google Calendar and Time Management Technology

Embark on a journey into the future of Google Calendar and time management technology. Explore the potential advancements that will redefine how we organize, schedule, and optimize our time:

1. Augmented Reality Integration:

- **Envisioning the Future:** Imagine a future where Google Calendar integrates with augmented reality (AR) devices. Visualize your schedule in a 3D space, providing an immersive and intuitive experience.

2. Predictive Intent Recognition:

- **Envisioning the Future:** Anticipate a future where machine learning evolves into predictive intent recognition. Google Calendar not only responds to commands but predicts your scheduling intentions based on subtle cues.

3. Biometric Authentication for Calendar Access:

- **Envisioning the Future:** Picture a future where biometric authentication, such as facial recognition or fingerprint scans, grants access to your calendar. Enhance security while ensuring convenient access.

4. Real-Time Collaboration Enhancements:

- **Envisioning the Future:** Envision real-time collaboration enhancements. Collaborators seamlessly contribute to shared calendars, make live updates, and engage in synchronized scheduling.

5. Advanced Natural Language Understanding:

- **Envisioning the Future:** See a future where natural language understanding reaches unprecedented levels. Google Calendar comprehends nuanced commands, colloquial language, and even emotional context for precise scheduling.

6. Quantum Computing for Scheduling Optimization:

- **Envisioning the Future:** Ponder a future where quantum computing transforms scheduling optimization. Complex algorithms process vast amounts of data in real-time, offering unparalleled efficiency in managing intricate schedules.

7. Cross-Platform Integration with Wearables:

- **Envisioning the Future:** Envisage seamless cross-platform integration with wearables. Smartwatches and other wearable devices provide instant access to Google Calendar, allowing for discreet and efficient scheduling.

8. Cognitive Load Reduction Techniques:

- **Envisioning the Future:** Imagine the integration of cognitive load reduction techniques. Google Calendar employs design principles and AI to minimize mental effort in managing and interpreting your schedule.

9. Emotionally Intelligent Scheduling:

- **Envisioning the Future:** Explore emotionally intelligent scheduling. Google Calendar takes into account your emotional state, adjusting the schedule to enhance well-being and productivity.

10. Hyper-Personalized Calendar Experiences: - Envisioning the Future: Delve into hyper-personalized calendar experiences.

Every aspect of Google Calendar—from colors to reminders—is tailored to individual preferences for a truly unique user experience.

11. Integration with Emerging Productivity Tools: - **Envisioning the Future:** Witness integration with emerging productivity tools. Google Calendar seamlessly connects with cutting-edge apps and platforms, ensuring users stay at the forefront of productivity trends.

12. Calendar Gamification for Engagement: - **Envisioning the Future:** Explore calendar gamification strategies. Users are motivated to adhere to schedules through game-like elements, earning rewards for meeting goals and maintaining a balanced calendar.

13. Proactive Health and Well-Being Features: - **Envisioning the Future:** Consider proactive health and well-being features. Google Calendar incorporates insights from health and fitness trackers, adjusting schedules to promote physical activity, breaks, and overall wellness.

14. AI-Driven Smart Suggestions: - **Envisioning the Future:** Picture AI-driven smart suggestions that go beyond scheduling. Google Calendar anticipates your needs, offering recommendations for activities, learning opportunities, and personal development.

15. Sustainable and Eco-Friendly Scheduling: - **Envisioning the Future:** Embrace sustainable and eco-friendly scheduling practices. Google Calendar incorporates environmental impact considerations, suggesting eco-conscious meeting times and travel options.

16. Universal Calendar Standards: - Envisioning the Future: Visualize the establishment of universal calendar standards. Google Calendar seamlessly interacts with calendars from different platforms, fostering interoperability and reducing scheduling complexities.

In the future landscape of Google Calendar and time management technology, innovation knows no bounds. These possibilities hint at a future where scheduling becomes not just efficient but deeply intuitive, personalized, and aligned with individual well-being.

CONCLUSION

As we wrap up this comprehensive journey into the realm of time management and scheduling, you've not only become familiar with the intricate features of Google Calendar but have also gained insights into the art and science of optimizing your time.

From the foundational understanding of why Google Calendar is an invaluable tool to the intricate details of event creation, customization, and collaboration, each chapter has equipped you with the knowledge to wield this digital scheduler with finesse. You've explored advanced functionalities, tapped into the potential of voice commands and smart assistants, and witnessed the transformative power of machine learning in shaping the future of time management.

In the realm of Google Calendar, your ability to orchestrate a symphony of events, meetings, and personal commitments has reached new heights. The integration of extensions, add-ons, and futuristic technologies ensures that your scheduling experience is not just efficient but tailored to your unique preferences and needs.

As you embark on your journey to master time, remember that Google Calendar is more than just a tool; it's a companion on your quest for productivity, balance, and success. Whether you're a seasoned professional, a student navigating deadlines, or anyone striving to make the most of each day, Google Calendar stands as a reliable ally in the pursuit of better time management.

As technology evolves and calendars become smarter, the potential for innovation in time management is boundless. The future holds promises of intuitive interfaces, augmented reality integrations, and emotionally intelligent scheduling—all designed to enhance your daily life.

So, as you continue to refine your scheduling skills and adapt to the ever-changing landscape of productivity tools, may your journey be marked by efficiency, balance, and the fulfillment of your goals. Let Google Calendar be the compass guiding you through the complexities of time, empowering you to make every moment count.

Here's to mastering your time, achieving your aspirations, and creating a calendar that reflects the rhythm of a well-lived life. Happy scheduling!

Printed in the USA
CPSIA information can be obtained
at www.ICGtesting.com
LVHW010200070624
782572LV00018B/249

9 798223 426400